FINAL FRENCH STRUGGLES IN INDIA

And on the Indian Seas

FINAL FRENCH STRUGGLES IN INDIA

And on the Indian Seas;

INCLUDING AN ACCOUNT OF THE CAPTURE OF THE ISLES OF FRANCE AND BOURBON, AND SKETCHES OF THE MOST EMINENT FOREIGN ADVENTURERS IN INDIA UP TO THE PERIOD OF THAT CAPTURE

COLONEL G . B. MALLESON, C.S.I.

GYAN

Published by

Gyan Publishing House
5, Ansari Road
Daryaganj, New Delhi-110002
Phone: 011-47034999, 9811692060
E-mail: books@gyanbooks.com

Distribution Network
gyanbooks.com
India, USA, Canada, UK, Australia, France

ISBN: 978-81-212-9282-5 (PB)
First Published, 1884

2nd Impression 2023

Printed at: Gyan Press, Delhi.

FINAL FRENCH STRUGGLES IN INDIA

Author: COLONEL G . B. MALLESON

FINAL FRENCH STRUGGLES

IN

INDIA.

FINAL FRENCH STRUGGLES IN INDIA

And on the Indian Seas;

INCLUDING AN ACCOUNT OF THE CAPTURE OF THE ISLES OF FRANCE AND BOURBON, AND SKETCHES OF THE MOST EMINENT FOREIGN ADVENTURERS IN INDIA UP TO THE PERIOD OF THAT CAPTURE.

WITH AN APPENDIX
CONTAINING AN ACCOUNT OF THE EXPEDITION FROM INDIA TO EGYPT IN 1801.

BY

COLONEL G. B. MALLESON, C.S.I.

AUTHOR OF THE "HISTORY OF THE FRENCH IN INDIA,"
"HISTORICAL SKETCH OF THE NATIVE STATES OF INDIA."

"The sun, the soil, but not the slave, the same
Unchanged in all except its foreign lord."
Childe Harold.

NEW EDITION.

LONDON:
W. H. ALLEN & CO., 13 WATERLOO PLACE,
PALL MALL. S.W.

1884.

DEDICATION.

DEAR MRS. SPENCER,

You may perhaps remember our conversations on the subject of my historical writings when you were staying with me on the Nílghiri Hills nearly twenty months ago. You then expressed your surprise that—considering the careers, full of strange and varied incident, of the sailors and adventurers who followed Dupleix and Lally in the struggle against the English—I had not continued and completed my History of the French in India. I was unable at the moment to take up your idea; but some months later I made it my own. That idea has now developed into a book, and the book is about to appear. Considering the circumstances of its origin, you will not, I feel assured, think me too presuming if I now ask you to accord to the young aspirant the privilege of introduction to the public under the auspices of your favour and of your protection.

Believe me,

Dear MRS. SPENCER,

Very sincerely yours,

G. B. MALLESON.

27, WEST CROMWELL ROAD,
1st *February*, 1878.

To MRS. ALMERIC SPENCER.

CONTENTS.

CONTENTS

INTRODUCTION.

The present work supplies a suppressed chapter of Anglo-Indian history. It undertakes, that is to say, to describe, in detail, the final struggle of the French, terminating in September, 1783, for empire in Southern India; the successful efforts of the same nation during the wars of the Revolution and the Empire to destroy British commerce in the Indian Seas; the suppression of those efforts accomplished by the capture of the Isles of France and Bourbon. It concludes with a sketch of the most famous adventurers who strove, often successfully, to train and discipline on the European model the soldiers of those native princes who, towards the close of the last century, seemed the most likely to come into hostile contact with the British.

It is strange, indeed, that in the standard English histories of India these later efforts of England's most persistent rival should have been dismissed in a few lines. It is stranger still when we consider how formidable those efforts appeared to contemporary writers, how nearly they approached success, how injuriously they did affect Anglo-Indian interests. The author of a book called *Transactions in India*, published in 1786, describes in clear and vivid language events in which he himself was an actor, and he paints the effect produced on the minds of the English by the daring exploits of Suffren. The French version of the same story, differing only in unimportant details, and styled *Histoire de la dernière guerre*, was published in 1787. Colonel Wilks, who wrote his admirable history of Southern India in the early days of the present century; who was in India when Suffren fought his five battles with his English rival and when Stuart was reduced to extremities at Kadalúr, describes in eloquent and impartial language the dangers incurred by the Presidency of Madras in 1783, and how it was saved from those dangers only by the timely suspension of arms which preceded the Treaty of Versailles.

These are, so to speak, the contemporary records of the period. The case for the English is stated in the *Transactions*, that for the French in the *Histoire*, and the events they record are summarised by an English writer, likewise an eye-witness. Yet the reader of the earlier editions of Mill's *History of India* would rise from the perusal of his description of the war terminated in 1783, and of its details, without the smallest suspicion that the supremacy of the English in Southern India had been greatly endangered. The account is more than meagre. It induces a belief that important events were unimportant. In a word, it suppresses the point of the subject of which it professes to treat.

A writer so honest and so conscientious as the late Professor H. H. Wilson could not pass over this omission without notice. The foot-note in which he gives to the subject its true point, although short, is most suggestive. "It seems probable," he writes, "that but for the opportune occurrence of peace with "France the South of India would have been lost "to the English. The annihilation of the army at "Cuddalore would have been followed by the siege "of Madras, and there was little chance of defending "it successfully against Tippoo and the French." The conclusion arrived at by Professor Wilson is so fully borne out by the facts of the case that the omission of details referring to those facts by the writers of the standard histories of India is very difficult to account for.

Some of my friends, indeed, who read a portion of this book in the pages of the *Calcutta Review,* have not hesitated to tell me that they regard as unpatriotic the attempt of an Englishman to search out and record events which may contrast favourably a rival nation with his own. But history is either a record of events which have happened or it is romance. If it assume to be a record of events which have happened it must record the evil as well as the good, misfortune as well as gain, defeat as well as victory. No one will dispute this broad axiom. But, to take a narrower view, it may with confidence be affirmed that the truly patriotic writer is he who does not attempt to hide the shortcomings of his own countrymen or the virtues of their enemies. It is the writer who attempts to lessen the merits of the enemy who is really guilty of want of patriotism. For, if the enemy were as contemptible as he is often described to have been by the purely insular writer, the merits of those who conquered him need not have been very considerable.

In attempting then to restore a suppressed chapter

of Indian history, in which the French navy appears to very considerable advantage, and a French admiral contesting the seas not unequally with an English admiral, finally out-manœuvres and beats him; in which events are recorded which all but upset English domination in Southern India; whilst I narrate facts which bring into strong light the virtues of individual Frenchmen, I relate the history of a struggle which ended in the triumph of England. There must have been some English virtues counterbalancing the French virtues, or some French defects greater than the French virtues, to enable the English to gain that triumph. For, by the admission of contemporary writers, our countrymen were reduced to extremities when, as if by the stroke of a magician's wand, they recovered all that they had lost. For the virtues and the defects, so nearly balancing each other on either side, I must refer the reader to the story itself. If success be a criterion of merit it is clear that the balance must, on a general consideration, be in favour of England.

The second Book is devoted to the description of a later attempt on the part of the French of a very different character indeed, but equally directed against

English interests. I allude to the efforts made by their privateers to destroy British commerce in the Indian seas; the success of those efforts; and, finally, the capture of the islands which had nurtured the daring corsairs, and whence they made their spring on the merchantmen of their rivals. It happened that whilst engaged in writing this portion of my book (1877) a debate occurred in the House of Commons on the subject of privateering. It would appear that there are some who still believe that by continuing to adhere to those stipulations of the Treaty of Paris which abolished privateering, England is placing herself at considerable disadvantage with other nations. I cannot but think that the perusal of my book will have the effect of changing the views of those who entertain this opinion. The note I have appended to page 81 shows that during the five years from 1793 to 1797 inclusive, whilst the French privateers captured 2266 English merchantmen, the English captures from her rival amounted only to 375! And this mainly happened, be it remembered, after Lord Howe's victory had annihilated the French navy, when England was the undisputed mistress of the seas. Is it possible to question the evidence offered by these figures that the nation which carries the largest amount of the commerce of the world must always be the chief sufferer from privateers?

If, indeed, further evidence to the same effect be required it will be found in the pages which follow the note I have quoted. The losses suffered by English traders in the Indian seas during the first sixteen years of the war were computed by millions. That these losses were caused by French privateers is not only shown in the text but is borne out by the fact that when, by the capture of the nest whence the corsairs sallied out to burn and to destroy, privateering was suppressed, the English merchantship was able to pursue her way in safety. The damage effected on the commerce of England by the light squadrons and single ships of her enemy was small. The privateers did all the mischief, and, as I have said, that mischief ceased when those daring cruisers were deprived of a base of operations.

If the advice urged by Marquess Wellesley in 1800-1 had been followed the depredations upon British commerce in the Indian seas would have ceased at a much earlier period. It was the rejection of that advice which caused to the British mercantile community those losses which, I have already stated, were to be counted by millions. When, ten years later, convinced against his will, Lord Minto, following in the lines of the great Marquess, carried out his views, the capture of the islands was found to be an operation comparatively easy, effected with but little bloodshed, and with a force which, large in comparison with the number of the defenders, was yet considerably smaller than the authorities both in England and in India had deemed necessary. The second Book, which professes to tell the story of the most famous of the privateers, fitly concludes then with the account of the successful expedition against the islands which were their home. From a national point of view the results are not dissimilar to those arrived at in the first Book. We see evidences of the same gallantry on the part of individual Frenchmen, and yet a conclusion favourable to England.

In the third Book I have endeavoured to give some detail of the careers of those foreign adventurers who disciplined and trained the armies which contested India with England at Aligarh, at Dehli, at Laswári, at Assaye, and at Argaum. There can be no question that in the last quarter of the last century there was in India scarcely any limit to the ambitious aspirations of an European adventurer who might possess even ordinary ability. When we see how men like Thomas and Perron, both originally common sailors, both devoid of abilities of the first-class, rose to the front rank; how one became the independent ruler of a principality, and the other governed, for Sindia, a portion of India comprehending roughly the country now known as the North-west Provinces; we gather an idea of the relative practical character of the European and the Asiatic at that epoch. But the sketches of the lives of these adventurers are not less interesting from another point of view. They give a remarkable insight into the mode of administration peculiar to the natives of Hindostan. Reading them, we can form some idea of the condition to which the whole of India would have been reduced, had Lake been beaten at Laswárí and Wellesley at Assaye. We can see how intrigue ruled supreme; how moral character went for nothing; how audacity, recklessness, corruption, always triumphed; how combined in one man, they were irresistible. The sense entertained by the natives themselves of the condition of life and property at that period is clearly shown in the proverb which has survived in some parts to the present day; "The buffalo is to the man who "wields the bludgeon." In my humble opinion, formed after a service in India of thirty-five years, during which I have mixed freely and on the most intimate terms with the natives, the seventy odd years which have intervened between the battle of Laswárí and the present day have wrought no considerable change in the general character of the people. Not that amongst them there have not been, and are not, men of the highest moral character; whose friendship is an honour, who know what is right and who act up to their knowledge. But these men form an inconsiderable minority. In a time of confusion they would be swept away. The love of intrigue still survives, and I write my own personal experience when I state that in the present decade, as much as in any that preceded it, intrigue uses falsehood and slander to move from high places men who strive earnestly and with all their power to eradicate those blots in the native character which were the curse of past generations.

In the last pages of this third Book I have endeavoured to show how in consequence of these vices it was inevitable that India should fall under the domination of a foreign master, and how the course of events caused that foreign master to be British. No one can deny that, however dimly the ultimate consequences may at the time have been foreseen by our countrymen, we fought for the position which we now occupy. It was with design that we crushed the hopes of the French; with design that we conquered Bengal; with design that we subdued Tippú; with design that in 1802-3 we contested Hindostan with Sindia and Holkar. Then, apparently for the first time, alarmed at the empire at our feet, we attempted to hold our hand. We withdrew from the princes of Rájpútáná the protection which Marquess Wellesley had promised them. What was the consequence? Thirteen years of oppression, of tyranny, of misgovernment in its worst form in central and in western India; the licensed atrocities of Amír Khan, the robberies of the Pindáris, dire spoliation by Maráthá chieftains and their followers. In spite of ourselves we had again to step in. With the defeat and deposition of the Péshwa, the overthrow of the Maráthás and Pindáris, the Marquis of Hastings closed a campaign, which restoring British protection to Rájpútáná, placed us formally on the pinnacle we now occupy. Thenceforward we were forced to go onwards. We annexed the Panjáb, annexed Sind, and sucked in Sattárá, the dominions of the Bhonslá, and Oudh. Suddenly the overgrown army of mercenaries we had created, feeling its power, rose in revolt. Again did England designedly assert her supremacy. The mutiny crushed, we found ourselves face to face with a new order of things. Thenceforward there were to be no more annexations. But the crushing of the mutiny had been but a continuation of the policy of Clive, of Hastings, of Wellesley, of Hardinge, of Dalhousie—a continuation forced upon us, but still a continuation. We thus possess India by our own act; we took the responsibility upon ourselves, and we are morally bound by it. On whom else could we cast it, if we would? We would not make it over to any European power; we could not, without assuming the fearful responsibility of a terrible and inevitable future, resign it to a native prince! No—we have gained it and we must keep it. For my part

I regard India as the brightest jewel in the diadem of the Queen of England. I believe that the natives of India are not solitary in deriving benefit from their connection with England; that directly and indirectly England greatly gains by it. But upon this large question I shall not here enter.

We are in India and we must stay there; and that we are there for the benefit alike of the princes and the people is a fact which the wise and thoughtful Indian will be the first to admit. Many of them may perhaps have forgotten the days when their country was divided into armed camps, each led by a Pindári marauder or a Maráthá freebooter; when justice was openly bought, when no man could say in the day that his house would belong to him on the morrow, when human life was uncared for, and when readiness to commit the vilest crimes was a sure road to Court favour. But these are matters which it is well not to forget. Recalling them to the memory the thinking reader will draw a contrast between that Maráthá period of Indian history, peculiarly favourable to reckless and unprincipled adventurers, Native as well as European, and that which has succeeded it, when as a rule the buffalo is to the honest and frugal peasant, and when the higher appointments under Government fall to the intelligent, the well instructed, and the conscientious citizen.

One word as to the authorities upon which I have drawn. The deeds of Suffren have been painted by four eminent French writers, Hennequin, Canat, Trublet, and Roux. I have carefully compared the statements made by these biographers with Dr. Campbell's naval history of the period, with the accounts given by the authors of the *Transactions in India*, and of the *Histoire de la dernière guerre*, by Wilks (*History of Southern India*), and with the information procured for me from the naval archives of France. For the second Book, I am indebted mainly to Canat (*Histoire de Surcouf*), to Gallas (*Les Corsaires Français sous la Republique*), to the *Asiatic Annual Register*, and to the files of Indian papers of the last century which are stored up in the Public Library of Calcutta. The contents of the third Book are based mainly on the memoirs of de Boigne, on a very curious record of the services of his brother officers under native princes during the last century by Major Ferdinand Smith, on the

Asiatic Annual Register, and on the newspaper files above alluded to.

To the work as it stands I have added an Appendix, giving a plain didactic account of the expedition from India to Egypt in 1801. It is true that the events recorded in this Appendix have only an indirect connection with the main subject of the book. But the French occupation of Egypt may fairly be considered an integral part of the efforts made by France to disturb the supremacy of England in India. When, moreover, it is remembered that we live in a time when the Eastern question is the burning question of the day, I shall be excused for thinking that a plain statement of an expedition from India to Egypt organised by a Wellesley, carried into execution by a Baird, and approved of by a Wellington, may not be altogether out of place or out of season. My authorities for the account of this expedition are the *Life of Sir David Baird*, the memoirs of the *Comte de Noé*, the British despatches, and the *Asiatic Annual Register*.

G. B. MALLESON.

27, West Cromwell Road,
1st *February*, 1878.

BOOK I.

FRENCH MARINERS ON THE INDIAN SEAS.

I.

In the history of the French in India I have brought the story of the struggle for empire in the East of that gallant and high-spirited people to the year 1761. From that date the land contest really ceased. For although, in 1782, France did despatch a considerable force to aid Haidar Ali, the decrepitude of its leaders and the death of Haidar combined to render its efforts fruitless. From 1761, indeed, the French ceased to be principals in the contest. Thenceforth the adventurous sons of her soil were forced to content themselves with the position of auxiliaries to native princes. The foremost amongst them, levying contingents of their own countrymen, took service in the courts which showed the greatest inclination to resist the progress of the increasing power of the English. Thus the younger Lally, Law, Raymond, de Boigne, Perron, Dudrenec, and many others became the main supports upon which Haidar Ali, the Nizam, Sindia, and Holkar rested their hopes for independence, if not for empire. But, after all, although in many cases these adventurers accomplished much in the way of organising resistance to the English, they did not succeed in their own secret views. They failed entirely to resuscitate the dream of successful rivalry to England. One by one they disappeared before the steady advance of the foe they had once hoped to conquer. Sometimes, as at Haidarabad, dismissed on the requisition of an English governor; again, as in 1802, beaten by the English general, they gradually renounced the cause as hopeless, and finally ceased to pursue the struggle. The hopes which had glimmered but very faintly after the death of Haidar, which had again been somewhat rekindled by the prudent measures of Mádháji Sindia, were dealt a fatal blow by Lord Lake at Aligarh and at Dehli, and were finally crushed by that stalwart soldier on the field of Láswárí.

But there was another element upon which the fortunes of France still flourished even after the blow dealt at her in 1761. Strange, indeed, it was, that during the contest which terminated in that year, she had never sent simultaneously to the field of action a capable general and a capable admiral. It is true that La

Bourdonnais combined both qualities in his own person, and the great things he had then been able to effect ought to have served as an example for the times that were to follow. But they did not. La Bourdonnais' stay in the Indian seas was short. He was succeeded by the feeble Dordelin. And subsequently, when the Government of Louis XV. made the greatest effort France had till then made to establish an empire in India; when it sent out a general who had won distinction on the battle-fields of Flanders, and soldiers who had helped to gain Fontenoy and Laffeldt, it selected as the colleague of the general an admiral of whom it has been written that "to an unproductive brain he added infirmity of purpose."

Subsequently to the capture of Pondichery in 1761, the position was reversed. When, eighteen years later, Bussy, gouty, infirm, and whom self-indulgence had made halting and undecided, was sent to command the land forces, he had as his naval colleague a man whose name, covered with an eternal ray of glory, still shines as one of the most illustrious, if not the most illustrious, in the naval annals of France. I allude to Pierre André de Suffren.

The Treaty of Paris, signed on the 10th February 1763, had restored Pondichery to France, but it was a Pondichery dismantled, beggared, bereft of all her influence. During the fifteen years which followed this humiliating treaty, Pondichery had been forced to remain a powerless spectator of the aggrandisement of her rival on Indian soil. Even when, in 1778, the war was renewed, the Government of France was but ill prepared to assert a claim for independence, still less for dominion, in Eastern and Southern India.

The natural results followed. Chandernagor fell without a blow (10th July 1778). Pondichery, ably defended for forty days against vastly superior forces by its Governor, Bellecombe, surrendered in the month of September following; the fleet commanded by M. de Tronjoly,—a feeble copy of Count d'Aché,—abandoned the Indian waters without even attempting to save Mahé. All seemed lost. The advantages gained by the English appeared too great to be overcome; when the marvellous energy of Haidar Ali, the Mahomedan ruler of Mysore, gave a turn to events which upset the most carefully laid calculations, and communicated to his French allies the most brilliant hopes.

On the 4th April 1769 Haidar Ali had dictated peace to the English under the walls of Madras. By one of the articles of this treaty the contracting parties bound themselves to assist each other in defensive wars. But when, during the following year, Haidar was attacked and was hardly pressed by the Márhátás, the English refused their aid. Haidar never forgave this breach of faith.

When, therefore, some nine years later, he saw the English embroiled alike with the French and the Márhátás, Haidar resolved to take his revenge. He first sent to the English an intimation that he should regard an attack on the French settlement of Mahé, contiguous to his own possessions on the western coast, as equivalent to an attack upon himself. The English notwithstanding took Mahé and endeavoured apparently to pacify the ruler of Mysore by sending to him ambassadors charged with presents. These latter were however little calculated to produce such an effect. They consisted of a pigskin saddle and a rifle which it was found impossible to load. Haidar returned them with contempt, and prepared for war.

His first efforts in the autumn were eminently successful. Outmanœuvring the English general, Munro, he defeated and took prisoners (9th and 10th September, 1780) a detachment of 3720 men, of whom upwards of 500 were Europeans, under the command of Colonel Baillie, at Perambákam. He then captured Arcot and some minor places.

But the ruler of Mysore had not been unmindful of the French alliance. Early in the year he had intimated to the representatives of that nation in India his determination to strike a decisive blow at their rivals,—a blow which must be fatal, if the French would only sufficiently aid him. But the ministers of Louis XVI. were not alive to the importance of the stake to be played for. In that year, when England was engaged in a life and death struggle with her own children in America, a fleet under Suffren and 3000 men under a skilled leader such as De Boigne, would have sufficed to clear of her rivals the whole country south of the

Vindhya range. But though roused by the exhortations of Haidar, and catching, though dimly, a feeble idea of the possibilites before her, France, instead of sending a fleet and an army to India, contented herself with the despatch of a squadron and a regiment to guard the isles of France and of Bourbon, which the English had not even threatened.

This squadron, commanded by M. Duchemin de Chenneville, found on its arrival at its destination that the French islands were perfectly well protected by the small detachment of vessels commanded by the French admiral on the Indian station, the Chevalier d'Orves. This officer, who had succeeded de Tronjoly, at once assumed the command of the new arrivals. He had then at his disposal six serviceable men of war, one frigate, and two corvettes. It was not a large fleet, but it carried with it one of the finest regiments in the French army, a regiment such as, if landed in India, should have sufficed to render the campaign of 1781 decisive.

A glimmering of the chances thus possibly awaiting him seems to have decided d'Orves to take this small fleet and this regiment to the Coromandel coast. He sailed then from the islands on the 14th October and sighted the coast near Kadalúr on the 25th January following (1781.) Before referring to his subsequent conduct, let us take a glance at the position of affairs on the mainland on that date.

Haidar, having outmanœuvred Munro, beaten Baillie,

and captured Arcot, had laid siege to Ambúr, Vellor, Wandewash, Permacól, and Chinglepat. The first named of these places surrendered on the 13th January, but on the 18th, Haidar, having received intelligence that the new English general, Sir Eyre Coote, had left Madras the previous day, with the intention of attacking him, raised the siege of the other places, and massed his forces. Haidar at first manœuvred to cut off Sir Eyre Coote from Madras, but Coote, careless of this, marched upon Pondichery—the inhabitants of which had shaken off the English yoke, and had begun to arm the natives—revictualling the fortified places on his route. Haidar turned, and, following, overtook him on the 8th February, cutting him off from the country inland. As they approached Kadalúr, marching in almost parallel lines, Haidar caught a glimpse of the French fleet under d'Orves, guarding the coast, and preventing the possibility of any supplies reaching the English by sea. At last, he thought, he had them. Coote possessed only the ground on which his army marched. He was between the sea guarded by d'Orves, and the grain-producing country shut out from him by Haidar. Sir Eyre Coote has recorded his opinion as to the fatal nature of his position. There seemed but one chance open to him, and that was that Haidar might be tempted to fight him. He tried then every expedient to induce that warrior to quit his lair. But the Asiatic was far too wary. He knew that, barring accidents, his enemy must surrender without firing a shot.

Haidar, meanwhile, had communicated with d'Orves and had begged him to land the regiment he had on board. He had pointed out to him likewise all the advantages of his position, the fact that the last army of the English was at their joint mercy, and that Madras was guarded by but 500 invalids.

Never had France such an opportunity. It was an absolute certainty. There was neither risk nor chance about it. The English fleet under Sir Edward Hughes was off the western coast. D'Orves had but to remain quietly where he was for a few days and the English must be starved into surrender. Sir Eyre Coote saw it; Haidar Ali saw it; every man in the army saw it; every man in the fleet saw it, excepting one. That man was d'Orves himself. Of all the positions in the world that one which most requires the possession of a daring spirit is the command of a fleet. That Government is guilty of the greatest crime which sends to such a post a man wanting in nerve, deficient in self-reliance. Once before had France committed the same fault by entrusting in 1757, to the feeble d'Aché, the task of supporting Lally. But at least d'Aché fought. His feebler successor, d'Orves, was not required to fight. He was required to ride at anchor in the finest season of the year, a time when storms are unknown in the Indian seas, and see an enemy starve,—and he would not.

D'Orves, described by his own countrymen as a man "indolent and apoplectic," saved Sir Eyre Coote. In spite of the protestations of Haidar, he sailed for the islands on the 15th February, taking away every man he brought with him, and having accomplished nothing. The English force at once obtained supplies from Madras.*

Haidar, thus left to himself, fought Coote on the 1st July at Chilambram, and, after a desperate contest, was beaten. On the 27th August following he again engaged Coote at Parambákam, and this time not unequally. Haidar, however, left the field to the enemy. On the 18th February following (1782) Colonel Braithwaite's detachment, after combating for three days, succumbed to the superior numbers of Tippú Sáhib. It was about the period of this last encounter that France appeared once again upon the scene, better though not perfectly represented; for while she entrusted her fleet to the greatest of all her admirals, she committed the

* The Viscomte de Souillac, at that time Governor of the Isle of France, has thus recorded his opinion of d'Orves, in a memoir in the Archives of the French Navy: "By this astonishing obstinacy of M. d'Orves, which I reported to the ministry at the time, we lost an opportunity such as will never recur, of becoming absolute masters of the Coromandel coast. This army of Kadalúr (Sir Eyre Coote's) 14,000 strong, of which 3000 to 4000 were English, comprised all the troops the English had in this part of India. Madras could not have held out, and the junction of our forces with those of Haidar Ali would have enabled us to conquer Tanjore and Masulipatam with all their dependencies."

An English writer, the author of *Memoirs of the late War in Asia*, published in 1788, and who himself took part in the campaign, writes as follows :—"Had the French admiral left only two frigates to block up the road of Cuddalore, consequences might have happened as fatal to the interests of Great Britain in the East Indies, as flowed in North America from the convention of Saratoga."

charge of her army first to an incapable sailor, only to replace him by a gouty sexagenarian. But to recount the causes which led to this powerful intervention we must for a moment retrace our steps.

II.

STILL unconscious of the fact that the War of Independence in America offered them the rarest opportunity for striking a decisive blow at the English power in India, the French Government were nevertheless alive to the necessity of preserving from attack the Cape of Good Hope, then belonging to their allies, the Dutch, and of maintaining a respectable force in the Indian Seas. Early, then, in 1781, a squadron of five men of war* was fitted out, and on the 22nd March sailed from Brest, under the command of the Commandant de Suffren.

This illustrious sailor was born at St. Cannat in Provence on the 13th July, 1726, the third son of the Marquis de Suffren de Saint Tropez. Destined for the navy he entered that service in 1743, and in the *Solide*, of 74 guns, joined the French fleet in the Mediterranean. He took part in an engagement with the English fleet under Admiral

* They were:

Le Héros,	.. 74	Guns.	Commandant	de Suffren.
L'Annibal,	.. 74	,,	Capitaine	de Trémigon.
L'Artésien,	.. 64	,,	,,	de Cardailhac.
Le Vengeur,	.. 64	,,	,,	de Forbin.
Le Sphinx,	.. 64	,,	,,	du Chilleau.

Matthews. Transferred to the frigate *Pauline,* he again had several opportunities of displaying his courage. The same year, serving on board *Le Monarque,* he was taken prisoner. After the peace of Aix-la-Chapelle he was released, and proceeding to Malta became one of the Knights of the order of St. John of Jerusalem. During the Seven Years' War he took part in the siege and capture of Port Mahon (29th July, 1756), and was for the second time made prisoner at the combat of Lagos (1759). Returning to France after a captivity of two years, he was promoted to the command of the *Caméléon* of twenty guns, and sent to the Mediterranean to protect the French commerce. Subsequently, in the *Singe,* he so distinguished himself as to be promoted to the grade of commander (*capitaine de frégate*). The seven years which followed offered little occupation to his warlike nature. In 1772 he was promoted to the rank of pos captain (*capitaine de vaisseau*), and in 1778, in command of *Le Fantesque,* he joined the squadron under Count d'Estaing, sent to aid the colonists of America. In the campaign which followed he so distinguished himself that he was granted a pension and marked for future command. A short cruise with two men of war in 1780 added to his reputation alike as a daring and skilful sailor and an unsurpassed manager of men. When, therefore, it was decided to send a squadron to the Indian seas, the choice of the minister fell naturally upon one who had shewn himself the most promising captain in the royal navy of France.

Such had been the services of the man who was now starting with a squadron of five line of battle ships to maintain the honour of his country in the Eastern seas. Setting sail on the 22nd March, in company with the fleet destined for the American waters under the Count de Grasse, Suffren separated from that admiral at Madeira, and continued his course towards the Cape of Good Hope. He had under his charge seven transports conveying detachments of the regiment of Pondichery, and overlooking these was a corvette of 16 guns, *La Fortune.* He had it very much at heart to reach the Cape as quickly as possible, so as to anticipate the arrival there of Commodore Johnstone, who, he had been informed, had sailed for that place from St. Helena with thirty-seven ships of sorts.*

Commodore Johnstone had sailed from Spithead on the 13th March, 1781, with orders to attack the Dutch possessions at the Cape. Arriving at St. Iago, one of the Cape de Verde islands, he deemed it necessary to stop there in order to take in wood, water, and livestock for his voyage. He accordingly put into Porto Praya early in April.

It so happened that one of Suffren's men of war, the *Artésien,* had been originally destined for the fleet sailing to the American waters, and her supplies of

* The squadron consisted of one ship of 74 guns, one of 64, three of 50, and three frigates. The remainder were armed transports.

The names were the *Hero*, 74; the *Monmouth*, 64; the *Isis*, *Jupiter*, and *Romney* of 50 each. The three frigates carried each 32 guns, and the transports had 112 guns amongst them.—*Campbell's Naval History* water had been regulated accordingly. As the French squadron approached the island of St. Iago, the commander of that vessel, M. de Cardailhac, suggested to his chief the advisability of his putting into the bay of La Praya, in order to complete his supplies. Suffren assented, and ordered Cardailhac to stand in. At the same time, to guard against any possible danger, he followed in his track with the rest of the squadron.*

On the morning of the 16th April, favoured by a breeze from the north-east, the *Artésien* had just passed between the islands of Maio and St. Iago, when her captain discovered at anchor at the entrance of the roadstead an English vessel, and almost immediately afterwards there burst upon his view the thirty-seven ships of war and transports which Commodore Johnstone had brought from England. Cardailhac at once signalled to his commander that enemies were in sight.

It was a great opportunity for Suffren. He doubted not that the English were quite unprepared to receive him; that they were dreaming of nothing less than of an attack; that the crews would probably be dispersed in search of water and provisions. And this was actually the fact. Of the crews of the English vessels nearly

* Campbell (Naval History) states that the French had received "by some means or other" information that Johnstone had put into Porto Praya; but his statement is quite unsupported. The same reason which had prompted Johnstone himself to put in, and that reason alone, guided the movements of Suffren.

fifteen hundred were out foraging; and Commodore Johnstone himself so little expected an attack that he was at the moment engaged in giving directions for altering the position of some of his ships which had drifted too near to each other.*

Suffren did not forego his chance. Despatching *La Fortune* to collect and guard the transports, he, at half-past ten in the morning, led the way in the *Héros,* and standing in close to the shore, followed by the other ships of his squadron, he made for the largest English vessel, also called the *Hero*, and cast anchor between her and the *Monmouth.*

The concentrated fire of the English squadron was for a few moments directed on the daring invader; but very quickly the *Annibal* came to her aid, and diverted to herself much of the enemy's attention.

The *Artésien,* which was following, was not fortunate. The smoke of the combat caused her captain, Cardailhac, to mistake one of the armed transports for a man-of-war. He was about to board her, when he was shot dead through the heart. La Boixière who replaced him was incompetent. He, too, mistook another transport for a frigate. Whilst engaged in boarding her, the freshening breeze took both his vessel and his prize quite out of the line of fire.

The *Vengeur,* which had followed, went along the line of the enemy, exchanging broadsides, but her captain's order to anchor not having been attended to, she

* Campbell.

made the tour of the roadstead, and then quitting it, found herself unable to return.

The *Sphinx*, owing to the mistake or disobedience of her captain, did not anchor. She endeavoured to maintain her position by manœuvring, keeping up at the same time a heavy fire; but she rendered little effectual aid.

Suffren found himself then with two anchored vessels, and one unanchored, and therefore comparatively useless, engaged with the whole English squadron. The odds were tremendous, but he still possessed the advantage always given by a surprise, and he continued, for an hour and a half, to maintain the unequal combat. At last, when the *Annibal* had lost her main and mizen masts, and her captain had been disabled; when the *Héros* had received considerable damage in her rigging, and had lost eighty-eight men killed and wounded; and when all hope of effectual aid from the other three vessels of his squadron had disappeared, he deemed it advisable to discontinue the contest. Signalling, therefore, to the *Annibal* to follow him, he slowly sailed out of the roadstead, still keeping up a tremendous fire.

The *Annibal* essayed to follow him; but, as she passed between the *Hero* and the *Monmouth*, her remaining mast fell by the board. Fortunately the wind had shifted and was now blowing strongly from the south-west. She managed thus to rejoin, though slowly, her consorts outside.

It was about half-past twelve o'clock in the day when

Suffren reunited his squadron outside the harbour and began to repair damages. Three hours later Commodore Johnstone followed him and appeared inclined to attack in his turn. Suffren, however, placing the *Annibal* in the centre of his line, offered so bold a front, that the English commodore, whose ships, especially the *Isis*, had suffered severely, drew off and returned to La Praya.* Suffren then continued his voyage without molestation, and on the 21st June cast anchor in Table Bay. The convoy arrived nine days later.

Having landed his troops at the Cape; having secured the colony against attack; having completely repaired his damages, and having been joined by two corvettes, the *Consolante* and the *Fine*, Suffren sailed for the islands of France and Bourbon on the 28th August. He cast anchor in Port Louis on the 25th October following.

* Dr. Campbell states that Johnstone "pursued the French, but he was not able to overtake them." The French authorities, on the other hand, assert that their fleet put on so bold a front that Johnstone stayed his advance, although he was within two cannonshot of their ships. "It was only at night," says Roux, "that the French continued their route, lighting their fires to provoke the enemy to follow them. The English, who had the advantage of the wind, dared not accept the challenge, but returned precipitately to La Praya." It is clear, considering the disabled state of the *Annibal*, and that the English commodore had the advantage of the wind, that he could have forced an action had he desired to do so.

On his return to the roadstead, Commodore Johnstone recaptured the transport taken by *l'Artésien*.

Much has been said by English writers regarding the fact that the Cape de Verde islands were neutral ground. It is perfectly true, but in this respect the French only did as they had been done by. The harbour of Lagos, in which the vessel on board of which Suffren served in 1759 had taken refuge, was equally neutral ground, and yet the French had been attacked in it by the English.

He found there six men of war, three frigates, and some corvettes. But at their head was the indolent and incapable d'Orves, the same who, we have seen, had already thrown away the most splendid chance of establishing a French India! It was under this man that Suffren was to serve as second in command!

Meanwhile the French Government had tardily decided to make in 1782 an attempt which could scarcely have failed if hazarded in 1780. It had resolved to strike another blow, this time in concert with Haidar Ali, for domination in Southern India. With this object in view it had roused from his retreat the Marquis de Bussy, the man who in his youth and middle age had gained honour and glory and wealth in that fairy land, but who now, gouty, worn out, and querulous, was incapable alike of decision and enterprise.*

The designs of the Court of Versailles had been communicated early in the year to M. de Souillac, Governor of the islands, and it had been intimated that transports containing troops would gradually arrive at his Governorship, and that, concentrating there, they would proceed to India, escorted by a powerful fleet under the command of Count d'Orves. De Souillac, who was enterprising and patriotic, had at once set to work to organise a force with the resources at his command from among the colonists; and at the period of the arrival of Suffren, he had drilled and armed a corps of 2868 men. Bussy had

* Bussy was then only sixty-four years old; but twenty years of sloth and luxury had quite impaired his faculties.

not then arrived. De Souillac therefore conferred the command of this force upon M. Duchemin.

It was an unfortunate choice. Duchemin was a sailor rather than a soldier. But he was strong neither on the sea nor on the land. He was as weak mentally as physically. A terrible fear of responsibility acted upon a constitution unable to bear the smallest fatigue. A man of moderate abilities would have sufficed for the occasion. The abilities of Duchemin were not even moderate.

These 2868 men, well commanded, and escorted to a given point by Suffren, would have sufficed to give the preponderance to Haidar Ali in his struggle with the English. But moments were precious. The war with the American colonists still indeed continued, but many things presaged that its duration would not be long. It was necessary, then, that the French should strike at once, and should strike with vigour and precision.

Of this necessity no one was more convinced than the Governor of the islands, de Souillac. He hastened his preparations, so that on the 7th December, 1781, the French fleet, consisting of eleven men of war, three frigates, three corvettes, one fireship, and nine transports containing troops, was able to set out for its destination.

What was its destination? Suffren, with a precision natural to him, had advised that it should sail direct for Madras, and attempt to take that town by a *coup de main*. But the cautious and feeble d'Orves had overruled him. He would only proceed by degrees. He would feel his way. It was too much for him even to take a straight look at India. He therefore directed the fleet upon Trincomali.

But Providence had one good turn in store for the French. Happily for the success of the expedition d'Orves died on the way (9th February, 1782). He made over the command to Suffren who had just received the rank of commodore (*chef d'escadre*). Suffren at once altered the course to Madras.

Before this event had happened, Suffren himself in his ship, the *Héros*, had pursued and captured an English man-of-war of 50 guns, called the *Hannibal*. She was at once added to the French fleet under the title of *Le petit Annibal*. From the officers of this vessel Suffren learned, for the first time, that large reinforcements were on their way to the English squadron in the East.

Passing Pondichery, Suffren despatched to that town, in a corvette, Lieutenant-Colonel Canaple, with instructions to communicate at once to Haidar Ali the intelligence of his arrival and his hopes. On the 15th February, just three days before Colonel Braithwaite's detachment succumbed to Tippú Sáhib, his fleet came in sight of Madras.* Anchored in front of Fort St. George, and protected by its guns, he descried eleven † ships of war,—

* The currents and a southerly breeze had taken his squadron considerably to the north of Madras. Coming again under the influence of the N.-E. Monsoon he approached Madras from the north.

† Dr. Campbell mentions only nine. The other two were probably frigates.

the squadron of Sir Edward Hughes. Suffren formed his ships in line of battle till he arrived within two cannonshots of the English fleet. He then anchored and summoned all his captains on board the *Héros* to a council of war.

It must always be remembered that the fleet of M. de Suffren was escorting transports conveying a *corps d'armée*, and that it was a main object with him to land his troops and disembarrass himself of his transports before attempting an equal combat with the enemy. The proposal then of the captain of the *Fine*, M. Perrier de Salvart, to attack Sir Edward Hughes, lying as he was under the cover of the guns of Madras, appeared to him too hazardous. He determined therefore to direct the transports on towards Porto Novo, covering their course with his fleet.

In pursuance of this decision the fleet commenced its southward course that same evening. But as the breeze freshened, Suffren observed the English vessels hoist their sails and follow him. Rightly conceiving that their object was to cut off his transports, Suffren gave the order that these should range themselves between the shore and his fleet, covered by the corvette the *Pourvoyeuse*, and make all sail for Porto Novo, whilst the *Fine* should watch the enemy's movements.

In spite of these precautions, however, Sir Edward Hughes, favoured by the darkness of the night, glided unperceived between the French squadron and the transports. These latter crowded sail to escape, and when day broke they and their pursuers had sailed almost out of sight of Suffren's squadron. Suddenly, however, the look-out man on board the *Fine* signalled the enemy to the south. Immediately every sail was set, and the *Héros*, followed by the rest of the squadron, soon approached the pursuers and the pursued. Sir Edward, thus baulked of this prey,* hove to, and ordered the chase to be discontinued.

In the battle now about to engage, the French had the advantage of two ships, having eleven against nine of the English. Yet this advantage, great as it was, was balanced, partly by the superior organization of the English, partly also by the jealousy and dislike entertained towards Suffren by the officers of the ships which had joined him at the islands. The jealousy, so often evinced in the time of Dupleix, which could not subordinate personal feelings to duty, manifested itself in the manner now to be described in the course of the action.

The French fleet was formed into two divisions; the first was composed as follows:—

Le Héros	74	guns,	carrying the commodore's broad pennant.
L'Orient	74	,,	one of the ships brought from Port Louis.
Le Sphinx	64	,,	brought by Suffren from Brest.
Le Vengeur	64	,,	ditto ditto.
Le petit Annibal	50	,,	captured from the English.

* Dr. Campbell says vaguely that he captured "several of them;" but the French accounts shew that all the troops were disembarked subsquently at Porto Novo.

The second division, commanded by the captain of the *Annibal*, de Tromelin, consisted of :—

L'Annibal	74 guns,	brought by Suffren from Brest.
Le Sévère	64 ,,	,, from Port Louis.
L'Artésien	64 ,,	,, by Suffren from Brest.
L'Ajax	64 ,,	,, from Port Louis.
Le Brillant	64 ,,	,, ditto.
Le Flamand	54 ,,	,, ditto.

The armament amounted to 710 guns.

The English fleet was thus composed :—

The Superb	74 guns, Flagship.	*The Monmouth*	64 guns.
The Hero	74 ,,	*The Worcester*	64 ,,
The Monarch	74 ,,	*The Barford*	64 ,,
The Exeter	64 ,,	*The Isis*	54 ,,
The Eagle	64 ,,	or a total armament of 596 guns.	

It was half-past three o'clock in the afternoon before the wind, which was light and variable, allowed Suffren to approach his enemy. Seeing even then that some of his captains had not occupied the post assigned to them, he signalled to them to take the place in the line which each could reach the most quickly.

Rapidly advancing then, he exchanged a broadside with the *Exeter*, but noticing the flag of the English admiral, he directed the *Héros* towards the vessel that bore it, at the same time signalling to the second division to close within pistol-shot of the enemy.

The combat lasted from half-past three to seven o'clock in the evening. But it was not till quite the close of the action that all the French ships came into the line of fire. The entire first division consisting of five ships was engaged throughout; but of the second the *Flamand* and the *Brillant* alone came to close quarters, the remaining four, disobeying the direct orders of the commodore, keeping up only a distant fire.

On the part of the English the brunt of the attack was borne by the *Exeter* and the *Superb*. The former, fought splendidly by Captain King, was terribly riddled. Her loss in killed and wounded was very great. The *Superb*, too, suffered severely.

At seven o'clock the combat ceased as if by mutual consent. Darkness had come on, and Suffren was too ill-satisfied with the conduct of five of his captains to risk a continuance of the contest. Sir Edward Hughes on his side was well content that it should cease. He was expecting reinforcements from England and by bearing down to the south he was likely to meet them. An opportunity would then offer to renew the battle on more advantageous terms. Taking advantage then of the quiescent attitude of the enemy he made all sail to the south.

It is probable that on this occasion, for the first and only time in his life, Suffren missed a great opportunity. He had on the whole had the advantage in the action. He had reduced one of the enemy's ships to an almost sinking condition * and their losses had been heavier than his own.

* "At the close of the action when she (the *Exeter*) had been most dreadfully cut up, two fresh vessels of the enemy's squadron bore down upon her. The Master asked Commodore King what he should do withher under the circumstances. His reply was "there is nothing to be done butto fight tlll she sinks." Just at this moment the two French ships were recalled. *Campbell.*

He knew that the English were expecting reinforcements. Why then did he not promptly pursue them? He did not do so because he could not trust all his captains.

The following morning Suffren summoned his captains on board the *Héros*. Those inculpated promised better conduct for the future. The squadron then quietly pursued its course to Porto Novo. Here Suffren disembarked his troops, negotiated the terms of an alliance with Haidar Ali, and on the 23rd, having re-victualled his ships and been joined by one man-of-war and three frigates, sailed for the south, protecting some transports he was despatching to the islands, and hoping to meet again his English rival.

On the 8th April his wishes in this respect were fulfilled. With his twelve line of battle ships he sighted, on the morning of that day, the eleven ships composing the squadron of Sir Edward Hughes* standing for Trincomali. For three days they continued in sight, Suffren finding it impossible to force an action. But on the morning of the 12th, Hughes, changing his course to gain Trincomali, unavoidably gave the Frenchman the advantage of the wind. Of this advantage Suffren made prompt use.

The action began about half-past twelve o'clock. Seven of the French ships were immediately engaged. But two, the *Vengeur* and the *Artésien*, notwithstanding the repeated signals of the commodore, kept at a distance, and their example was for some time followed

* The French ships carried 972 guns; those of the English 737.

by the *Sévère*, the *Ajax* and the *Annibal*. At last these three came up, and the action became general.

In the early part of the day fortune seemed to incline to the French. The *Monmouth* was dismasted and compelled to quit the line, having had 45 men killed and 102 wounded. The *Superb* was greatly damaged. The English admiral then gave orders to the squadron to wear. By this manœuvre, the position of the rival fleets was reversed. Still, however, the battle continued; when suddenly at six o'clock a tremendous storm burst upon both fleets, enveloping them in darkness, and forcing them, close to a lee shore, to pay attention to their own safety. Suffren at once signalled to anchor.

In this battle the English lost 137 killed and 430 wounded; the French 130 killed and 364 wounded. The *Héros*, the *Orient* and the *Brillant* had suffered severely. Nevertheless the next morning Suffren offered battle to Sir Edward, but the English admiral, having a large convoy under his charge, declined it. Suffren then sailed southward, whilst the English squadron entered the harbour of Trincomali. As to the captains of the *Vengeur* and the *Artésien*, Captains de Forbin and de Maurville, Suffren reported their conduct to the Minister of Marine. Subsequently, it will be seen, he deprived them of their commands and sent them to France, where, on arrival, they were imprisoned.

A little more than a fortnight after this battle, Suffren brought his squadron into the anchorage of Batacola, a Dutch port in the island of Ceylon, about twenty leagues to the south of Trincomali, to which place the English squadron had repaired. By taking up this position Suffren gained all the advantage of the wind which was just beginning to set in from the south. He had previously despatched a brig, the *Chasseur*, to the islands to demand of M. de Souillac men and munitions of war, of which latter there did not remain to him a sufficient quantity for a single action.

Here, at Batacola, Suffren received despatches from France directing him to proceed to the islands to escort Bussy to the Indian coast.* But there were grave reasons which urged Suffren to defer obedience to these instructions. In the first place he could not place confidence in many of his captains. The senior next to himself, Captain de Tromelin, was a man whom he had reason specially to mistrust. To leave to such a man the charge of a squadron wanting in men and ammunition, at a time when an English squadron of almost equal force was ready to dispute with it the mastery of the Indian Seas, and when nearly 3000 French troops, but just landed, required the support of French ships, was a course which prudence and patriotism alike spurned. Suffren preferred then to take upon himself the responsibility of not obeying the minister's order. He justified this line of action in a letter to the Governor of the Isles of France and Bourbon.

* These despatches were brought to Suffren by Villaret-Joyeuse, subsequently distinguished as the admiral who, with a revolutionary fleet, fought the battle of the 1st June against Lord Howe.

Fortunately for France the Governor of the islands was a man endowed with a cool judgment, a clear understanding, and large and comprehensive views. He in his turn justified the action of Suffren to the Minister of Marine. After detailing the various reasons which would render the absence of Suffren from the scene of action not only inexpedient but dangerous to French interests, he thus concluded : "It may truly be affirmed that the course M. de Suffren has taken will save India and pave the way for the success of the Marquis de Bussy."

The French fleet remained in the anchorage of Batacola till the 1st June. It was a trying time for Suffren. His greatest enemies were the recalcitrant captains who were sighing for the luxurious diet, the graceful forms, and the smiling faces of the Isle of France. These offered a covert resistance to all the plans of their commodore. But Suffren saw through their motives, and being a plain speaker, he told them bluntly that he would rather sink the squadron before the forts of Madras than retire before Admiral Hughes. "If there are any," he added, "who have formed the conception of such an infamy let them give me their reasons and I shall know how to answer them." It was in putting down the intrigues formed by these men, in repairing and re-victualling his ships, in tending on the shore the sick and wounded, and finally in welcoming re-inforcement of men and munitions, that the six weeks at Batacola were spent.

Meanwhile the troops under the feeble Duchemin, disembarked at Porto Novo the 20th April, had begun their operations. It had been arranged between the French commodore and Haidar Ali that 6000 infantry and 4000 cavalry of the Mysore army should join the French force, and that these united should, under the command of the French general, act in concert with Haidar Ali, the latter furnishing supplies both in money and kind. These arrangements were quickly carried out. Haidar had wished that the Freneh *corps d'armée* should at once attack Negapatam, a most important town on the coast, and the capture of which could then have been easily effected. Duchemin, however, preferred the easier conquest of Kadalúr. This place surrendered on the 6th May. A junction was then effected with Haidar Ali, and the united armies besieged and took Permacól, and a few days later invested Wandewash.

Then occurred another instance of the crime of intrusting important military operations to a man without brains and without nerve. Probably in private life Duchemin was amiable and inoffensive. He was certainly not tormented by a constant desire to dare. These somewhat negative qualities ought to have engendered a doubt as to the possession of the sterner faculties which fit a man for command. It has indeed been conjectured that he might have owed his selection to there not being a better man on the spot. Yet, judging by results, such a surmise must be a libel on all and every one of the 2868 men he led to India.

Just imagine his position. The English had but one army in Southern India. That army consisted of about 12,000 men, of whom little more than 2000 were Europeans. It was commanded by Sir Eyre Coote, a man who had been very good in his day, but who was then utterly broken down in health. That army defeated, and Southern India would become Mysorean and French.

On the the other side was the army of Haidar Ali, 60,000 strong, flushed with victory over Braithwaite, and but just joined by about 2000* Frenchmen under Duchemin. For this army a defeat was comparatively unimportant; for the English had not the men to follow up the victory, and Haidar had another army to fall back upon. It was just the occasion when it was the policy of the English to avoid a decisive action, of the allies to force one on.

Yet, it is scarcely credible that, whilst the English general so far played into his enemy's hands as to offer battle to them, the French commander declined it. If success justifies the neglect of all rule, then, and then alone, was Coote warranted in offering battle. Defeat would have ruined him. Yet his part, at least, was a noble and a daring part. But what can justify Duchemin?

Look again at the position. Haidar Ali and Duchemin with an army of over 60,000 men were besieging Wandewash; Sir Eyre Coote thought that Wandewash must be saved at any price. He therefore advanced with his

* Deducting the sick in hospital.

army, 12,000 strong, and offered battle to the allies. His position was of no great strength. He had no advantages. He was over-matched in cavalry, in infantry, and in artillery. Haidar, old as he was, was eager to accept the challenge. Duchemin refused.

Why did he refuse? The fate of French India was in his hands. He had but to tell his countrymen to fight, as Frenchmen will fight, and, in all probability, Wandewash would have been the grave of the English. Why then did he refuse? It was an opportunity at which Suffren would have clutched, which the least of the generals of Napoleon would have made decisive. Unhappily for France, Duchemin was less than the least of her warrior children.

In reply to the urgent requisition of Haidar, Duchemin pleaded his health; he pleaded his instructions not to fight before the arrival of Bussy; he pleaded, not in words, but in a manner not to be misunderstood, his own innate incapacity.

Haidar Ali saw it—saw it with disdain. In compliance with the urgent solicitations of the Frenchman, he abstained from attacking Coote, and, raising the siege of Wandewash, retreated towards Pondichery, and occupied a strongly fortified position close to Kalinúr. But the loss of the opportunity chafed him. Such allies were useless to him. He determined to show them he could fight the English without them.

The occasion soon presented itself. Sir Eyre Coote, foiled in his endeavours to force on a battle before

Wandewash, determined to make an attempt on the magazines of Haidar at Arni. There were all his stores; there his supplies of ammunition and weapons of war. To surprise that place would in very deed give a deadly wound to his enemy. Coote resolved to attempt it. His chances seemed good, for he had gained over the commandant of Arni.

Coote set his army in motion for that purpose on the night of the 30th May. But Haidar had had good information and had penetrated his plan. Whilst then he sent by forced marches Tippú and his own French contingent under the younger Lally to protect Arni, he broke up from his camping ground at Kalinúr, and marched on the track of Coote, hoping to take him in rear. He did not even ask the opinion of Duchemin, but left him and his *corps d'armée* behind.*

Haidar Ali overtook the English force on the 2nd June just as they were in sight of Arni. The English leader was surprised. He had Tippú and Lally in front of him, and Haidar Ali in his rear. His troops were tired. Haidar had never had such a chance. But the skill of Coote and the valour of the English baffled him. By dexterous manœuvring Coote made it a day of skirmishing, in the course of which he captured one of Lally's guns stuck fast in the bed of the river. In his main object, however, Coote was baffled. Haidar saved Arni. Four days later Haidar took his revenge for the loss of

* To mark his sense of Duchemin's conduct Haidar suspended the supply of provisions to the French army during his own absence.

his gun by tempting the English into an ambuscade. They fell into the snare, and lost 166 men, 54 horses, and two guns. Haidar's loss was about 60 men. After this action Sir Eyre Coote returned to the vicinity of Madras. Haidar, unable to conquer the repugnance to action of Duchemin, proceeded to push on the siege of Vellor.

III.

It was whilst the events just recorded were progressing on land that intelligence from time to time reached Haidar Ali of the gallant contests which Suffren had been delivering on the sea. The enthusiasm of the tried. and gallant old warrior knew no bounds. "At "last," he said to his confidants, "at last the English "have found a master. This is the man who will aid "me to exterminate them: I am determined that two "years hence not one of them shall remain in India, "and that they shall not possess a single inch of Indian "soil." Then turning to the French agent in his camp, M. Piveron de Morlat, he begged him to write at once to his master, and to tell him of his own great desire to see him, to embrace him, to tell him how much he esteemed him for his heroic courage.

Before this message could reach the French commodore, Suffren had sailed with his refitted and augmented squadron in the direction of Kadalúr. It had been his original intention to do the work which Duchemin had declined to attempt, *viz.*, to take possession of Negapatam, which would have formed an important depôt for the operations of the land and sea forces. But the course of events induced him to change his determination.

The French fleet, consisting of twelve ships of the line and four large frigates, sailed first to Tranquebar, and then, making several captures *en route*, arrived, on the 20th June, at Kadalúr. Here for the first time Suffren became acquainted with the misconduct of Duchemin. Resolved, by some daring measure, to atone for the shortcomings of this incapable soldier, Suffren embarked on board his transports, besides siege materials, 1200 men of the line, 400 of the levies of the islands, two companies of artillery, and 800 sepoys, intending to make a dash at Negapatam. He was on the point of sailing when intelligence reached him that the English fleet, emerging from Trincomali, had passed Kadalúr, and was bearing up northward in the direction of the place which he had hoped to surprise.

Disappointed, but still determined, Suffren at once set sail in pursuit of the enemy. Coming in sight, on the 5th July, of Negapatam, he beheld the English fleet lying at anchor in the roadstead. Determined at all hazards to force on an action, Suffren signalled to clear decks and to be ready to anchor. His own ship, the *Héros*, was leading, when at three o'clock, a sudden squall caused to the *Ajax*, which was following, the loss of her main and mizen topmasts. These, and other damages, almost as serious, forced her to drop out of the line. The squall settling into a steady breeze gave the English admiral the advantage of the wind. He accordingly weighed anchor and stood out to sea. That night the two fleets anchored within two cannonshots of each other.

When the morning of the 6th July broke, the first care of the French commodore was to ascertain the condition of the *Ajax*. His rage may be imagined when he found that the necessary repairs remained uncompleted. The rage was increased to fury when he received from her captain a request that his vessel might be allowed to stand in for the nearest roadstead, and this in the presence of an enemy and when an engagement was impending! He refused absolutely.

Meanwhile the English admiral, finding the enemy of about equal strength with himself,* determined to use his advantage of the wind and to force on an engagement. At ten minutes past seven, then, he formed line ahead, and signalled to his captains that each ship should bear down as directly as possible upon her opponent and endeavour to bring her to close action. Suffren on his side tacked, putting the head to the wind, in order to form a new line. As he did this, he had the mortification to see the captain of the *Ajax* stand right away from him.

It was not till about half-past nine o'clock that the English ships came within range of their enemy. Both fleets opened fire simultaneously at long distances.

* The French fleet consisted, besides the *Ajax* which took no part in the battle, of eleven ships of the line, carrying 706 guns, and of four frigates. The English had eleven line of battle ships, carrying 746 guns, and one frigate.

Soon, however, the fight closed. The *Flamand*, 50, drew upon herself the fire, which she returned, of the *Hero*, 74, and the *Exeter*, 64; whilst the *Annibal*, 74, engaged in a murderous conflict with the *Isis*, 56. Simultaneously the *Sévère*, 64, and the *Barford*, 74; the *Brillant*, 64, and the *Sultan*, 74; the French commodore's ship, the *Héros*, 74, and the English admiral's ship, the *Superb*, 74; engaged in an almost hand to hand encounter.

Of the other vessels it may be noted that the *Sphinx*, 64, fought the *Monarca*, 74; but the position of this latter, on the starboard quarter of the *Superb*, rendered it impossible for her to deliver any but an oblique fire. The *Worcester*, the *Monmouth*, the *Eagle*, and the *Magnamine*, which followed in her wake, could only form a line at an angle of forty-five with the French line. It followed that the fire between these and the *Petit Annibal*, the *Artésien*, and the *Vengeur* was at a long distance, whilst the *Bizarre* and the *Orient*, notwithstanding the efforts of their captains, remained in forced inaction. The *Flamand* was the first French ship to feel the weight of her two powerful antagonists. She managed, however, to forge ahead and clear herself, and they were in too crippled a condition to follow her. The *Brillant* at the same time was suffering much from the well-directed fire of the *Sultan*, when Suffren, signalling to the *Sphinx* to replace him alongside the *Superb*, came to her rescue. The fight was then renewed with extraordinary vigour; when at one o'clock the wind suddenly changed, and threw both the combating parties into disorder.

This change of wind, according to the English writers, saved the French fleet from certain defeat. The French on their side, whilst admitting the shameful conduct of some of their captains, contend that the battle was still uncertain, and that they were combating with equal chances when the wind came to part them. The state of affairs after the change of wind had operated, as stated by one of the English writers of the period, a decided partisan, shows, I think, that there could have been little to choose between the condition of the rivals. "After much manœuvring," he writes, "and the continuation of a partial engagement between such of the two fleets as came within reach of each other, the English admiral made the signal for the line of battle ahead, and was preparing, at half-past one o'clock, to renew the attack; but seeing, at two, the enemy standing in shore, and collecting their ships in a close body, while his were much dispersed, and several of them ungovernable, he relinquished that design, and thought only of getting into such a condition as should prove decisive to the service next morning. Then, however, the French were observed under sail, on their way to Cuddalore, while our fleet was utterly incapable of preventing or pursuing them."* If this does not imply that the English ships had been at least

* *Transactions in India.* London: 1786. Campbell says: "The action was obstinate, well fought, but indecisive."

as much damaged as their enemies in the previous encounter there is no meaning in language.

The French statement corroborates substantially the account from which I have just quoted. "Sir Edward Hughes," it relates, "abandoning to us the field of "battle, endeavoured to concentrate his ships between "Negapatam and Naoúr, whilst Suffren, lying to, and "seeing the English squadron disappear, gave orders to "anchor off Karikál, two leagues to windward of it."

Suffren himself attributed the indecisive nature of the action to the conduct of his captains. He accordingly placed under arrest and sent to France the following three of their number, *viz.*, M. de Maurville of the *Artésien*, for having on the 6th July aggravated the faults he had committed on the 17th February, the 12th April, and the 5th June; M. de Forbin, for having on this occasion rivalled his misconduct on the 12th April; and M. de Cillart for having unbecomingly hauled down his flag.* M. Bouvet, who had not brought the *Ajax* into action at all, was deprived of his command, whilst three other inferior officers were sternly reprimanded. Having rid himself of these worse than incapable captains, Suffren anchored in the roadstead of Kadalúr

* This occurrence is thus summarised from the French authorities: "In one of the isolated encounters *le Sévère* was sustaining a fierce combat with the *Sultan*. All at once, in spite of the proximity of *l'Annibal*, *le Sphinx*, and *l'Héros*, de Cillart ordered his men to haul down his flag. Fortunately his cowardice, which betrayed itself by unmistakeable signs, remained without result. Two officers rushed to him, and apostrophising him severely, rehoisted the flag and continued the combat."

and devoted all his efforts to repair the damages his ships had sustained in the action.

Yet, whilst actively engaged in this prosaic work, his brain, never idle, had conceived one of the most daring projects which ever entered into the head of a naval commander. Long had he noticed with envy the possession by the English of the only harbour on the eastern coast of Ceylon, capable of containing a large fleet, at the same time that it was strong enough to defy any hostile attack. He lay before Kadalúr in an open roadstead, liable to the storms of the ocean and the attacks of a superior force of the enemy. In this open roadstead he had to carry out all his repairs. The English admiral, he knew well, was about to be joined by the *Sceptre* of 64 guns and the *San Carlos* of 44. Were he to be attacked by the force thus increased to a very decided superiority, how could he effectually resist? Considerations of this nature pointed to the advisability of securing a harbour at once large, commodious, and safe. These advantages were possessed by Trincomali. Suffren then resolved to capture Trincomali.

It was a bold, almost an audacious venture. After the combat of the 6th July the English admiral had kept the sea for nearly a fortnight to the windward of Negapatam.* With his ships much battered and

* The only English writer who attempts to justify the English admiral's delay before Negapatam, the author of *Transactions in India*, says that the situation of the army *may have* rendered this inaction necessary. But there are no grounds for this supposition. The English army was then likewise in a state of complete inaction.

urgently needing repair it is not easy to imagine why Sir Edward Hughes wasted that precious fortnight in idle bravado. This at least is certain, that it gave Suffren the opportunity he was longing for.

The state of his vessels and the necessity for procuring ammunition rendered it impossible for Sir Edward Hughes to keep the sea for more than a fortnight. He steered then for Madras and reached that place on the 20th July. He at once took the necessary measures for the repairs of his fleet. Here also he was joined by the *Sceptre* and the *San Carlos.* Sir Edward Hughes thought, and he seemed to have reason for his opinion, that he had sufficient time before him. He knew to a great, though not to the fullest extent, the difficulties his rival had to encounter at Kadalúr. Had he known the whole truth, he would have felt still more confident, for, on the 30th July, ten days subsequently to his own arrival at Madras, the state of the French ships of war was so miserable, and the resources at the disposal of Suffren were so limited, that action for the remainder of the year seemed for them impossible.

On that date Suffren thus wrote to the Governor of the Isle of France, M. de Souillac: "I assure you it is " no easy matter to keep the sea on a coast, without " money, without magazines, with a squadron in many " respects badly furnished, and after having sustained " three combats. * * I am at the end of my resources. Nevertheless we must fight to gain Ceylon; " the enemy have the wind of us and we have so many

" slow sailers that there is little hope we shall gain that
" advantage. * * The squadron has 2000 men in
" hospital of whom 600 are wounded."

Even before thus writing Suffren had broken up his prizes and transports, and had demolished houses and other buildings in Kadalúr to provide himself with the means of repairing his damaged ships!

Whilst thus engaged in these important duties, intelligence reached Suffren (25th July) that the great sovereign of Mysore had arrived within a few miles of Kadalúr in the hope of seeing him and of concerting plans for the future. The French commodore at once despatched an officer of rank to congratulate Haidar Ali, and the next day he landed himself in state, to pay him a visit of ceremony.

His reception was magnificent. Met on landing by the principal nobles of Mysore, escorted by Haidar Ali's own bodyguard of European cavalry, he was greeted on the threshold of the state-tent by that prince himself. The appearance of Haidar Ali was the signal for a general presentation of arms on the part of the troops drawn up in battle array. The drums beat, the trumpets sounded, the attendants sang hymns recording the prowess of the French. Not a single mark of respect or of honour was omitted.

The interview lasted three hours. Towards the close of it Suffren suggested to Haidar that he should come down to the sea shore to look at the French fleet dressed out in his honour. But Haidar, who was suffering, and who did not care to undergo the exertion that would be necessary, replied that he "had left his camp for one "object only, that of seeing so great a man, and that "now that he had seen him there was nothing remain-"ing that he cared to see."

The two following days were spent in giving and receiving presents, and in arranging as to the operations which should take place on the arrival of Bussy. They were actually engaged in discussing this question, when intelligence was received of the arrival at Point de Galle of the advanced guard of Bussy's fleet under M. d'Aymar.

Bussy, in fact, had set out from Cadiz in December 1781 with two men-of-war, three transports, and a large convoy. His misfortunes set in early, The convoy was attacked, dispersed, and in part destroyed by English cruisers, so much so that only two ships laden with artillery joined him at the Cape.* He still, however, had the soldiers who had embarked on his three transports. Terrified, however, at a report that the English were about to attack the Cape with an army of 6000 men, he left there 650 of his small detachment. Sailing then to the islands, the perusal of the despatches just arrived from Suffren seemed to give him new courage. In concert, then, with the Governor, M. de Souillac, he detached under M. d'Aymar, two men of war, the *St. Michael*, 64, and the *Illustre*, 74, one frigate, the *Consolante*, and nine storeships, carrying 800 men and laden with supplies and ammunition, to

* Many subsequently made their way to the islands.

proceed at once to join Suffren, and to announce that he himself would shortly follow with the bulk of his troops.

It was of the arrival of this squadron at Galle that Suffren received information at Kadalúr on the 28th July, whilst still discussing affairs with Haidar Ali.

He lost no time in delay. Some preparations were still necessary. But these were soon completed, and on the morning of the 1st August, the French fleet leaving the roadstead in which it had patched up its repairs, fired a parting salute to the great warrior her commodore was never destined again to behold.

Suffren had two objects in view, the one avowed, the other concealed: the first to effect a junction with d'Aymar; the second to capture Trincomali: the first appeared certain; the second could only be accomplished by "great daring."

Passing Karikál, Naoúr, and Negapatam, the fleet arrived at Batacola, twenty leagues south of Trincomali, on the 9th August. Here it was joined by the *Bellona*, a frigate of 36 guns, just returning from an indecisive hand-to-hand encounter with the *Coventry*, 32. Her captain, M. de Pierrevert, a nephew of Suffren, had been killed in the action.

Suffren waited at Batacola till the 21st August, when he was joined by the *St. Michael* and the *Illustre*, escorting seven transports with troops and stores, and accompanied by the corvette *La Fortune*. Whilst lying at Batacola he received despatches from France and the islands. Amongst those from the latter was one from Bussy in which that general pointed out how much to be regretted it was that the French possessed no harbour on the eastern coast equal to Trincomali. It cannot be said that this letter decided Suffren, for his mind had been previously made up; but it is probable that this opinion of a man who had a great reputation on matters connected with India greatly strengthened his determination to strike for Trincomali.

The reinforcements brought by d'Aymar did not remain long in Batacola. One day was spent in distributing to the several ships the munitions and stores of which they were in need. The next day, 22nd August, the entire fleet set sail, and the same evening cast anchor in front of Trincomali. Early on the morning of the 25th Suffren, having well examined the fortifications, moved his fleet to the east of the forts protecting the town, with the intention to land there his troops, to the number of 2400. This was effected without opposition the same evening. On the 26th batteries were constructed to play on the eastern face of the fort. On the 27th, 28th, and 29th, fire was opened and continued until, on the evening of the last-named day, a breach had been effected in the fortifications. Early on the following morning Suffren summoned the commandant to surrender. After a long debate, the commanding officer, Captain Macdowel, seeing that further resistance was useless, agreed to give up the place on the condition that he and his troops should be transported to Madras and be free to serve in the war. The French then entered into possession.

Trincomali capitulated on the 31st August. It was occupied by the French on the 1st September. On the 2nd the fleet of Sir Edward Hughes appeared in sight of the place.

IV.

We have seen that Sir Edward Hughes, after delaying for nearly a fortnight before Negapatam, at last took his fleet to Madras to refit. He arrived there on the 20th July, and there he was joined by the *Sceptre* and *San Carlos*.

The damages which many of his ships had sustained were considerable, and he was forced to make extraordinary exertions to repair them. It had occurred to him that the French commander might take advantage of the state of his vessels, and the gain of a fortnight's time, to make an attempt upon Trincomali. To guard as much as possible against such an attempt, he despatched the *Monmouth* and the *Sceptre* with supplies of men and ammunition to that place.* Thinking this sufficient, his anxiety on the subject ceased. It was soon roused, however, to a greater extent than ever.

I have mentioned that the French frigate *Bellona* fought an indecisive action with the *Coventry* off Batacola; but I did not then state that the combating vessels had approached sufficiently near to that place to enable the

* These ships were descried by the French fleet on the 3rd of August off Negapatam. It is probable that they did not go further.

captain of the latter ship to see the whole French fleet at anchor. He at once crowded on sail to carry the news quickly to Madras. He reached Madras in the middle of August, and gave the first intimation to Sir E. Hughes of the dangerous proximity to Trincomali of his enemy. Sir Edward used all the despatch possible to hasten his departure for Ceylon. At length he set out, but, delayed by contrary winds, he arrived before Trincomali only to see the French flag flying on all the forts, and the French fleet at anchor in the bay.

Suffren saw, not unmoved, the English fleet in the offing. It was not necessary for him to go out and fight it, for he had succeeded to the fullest extent of his expectations. He had taken Trincomali. There were not wanting officers in his fleet to urge upon him to run no further risk. The party which, ever since his departure from the islands, had constantly endeavoured to thwart his measures, had been weakened but not annihilated, by the deportation to France of de Cillart, de Maurville, and de Forbin. The head of this party was his second in command, M. de Tromelin, captain of the ship *Annibal*. Supported by de St. Felix of the *Artésien*, by de la Landelle of the *Bizarre*, and others, de Tromelin urged upon the commodore the advisability of resting upon his laurels. "The issue of a combat," he said, "was uncertain, and might deprive them of all that "they had gained." Such was their ostensible reason; but it cannot be doubted that it was used to cover alike their jealousy of their chief, and their longing desire to return to the soft beauties of the Isle of France. As for de Tromelin, he had held back in every action, and it was a matter of surprise that he had not been deported with the others after the last engagement.

It is necessary to give this summary of the debates which preceded the action, because they exercised a momentous influence on the action itself.

Before giving a decisive answer to his peace-pleading captains, Suffren determined to ascertain the number of the enemy's vessels. He accordingly signalled to the frigate *Bellona* to reconnoitre. The *Bellona* in a very short space of time signalled back that there were twelve English ships. This decided Suffren. He had fourteen.* Turning to his advisers, he said, "If the enemy had "more ships than I have, I would abstain; if he had "an equal number, I could scarcely refrain; but as he "has fewer, there is no choice; we must go out and "fight him."

The fact is that Suffren saw, though his captains would not or could not see, that a grand opportunity, possibly the last, now offered to strike a decisive blow for dominion in Southern India. Could he but destroy,

* The French fleet consisted of *le Héros*, 74; *l'Illustre*, 74; *l'Orient* 74; *l'Annibal*, 74; *l'Artésien*, 64; *le Sévère*, 64; *le St. Michel*, 64; *le Brillant*, 64; *le Sphinx*, 64; *l'Ajax*, 64; *le Vengeur*, 64; *le Bizarre*, 64; *le Petit Annibal*, 50; and four frigates, carrying in all 1038 guns. The English fleet comprised the *Hero*, 74; the *Burford*, 74; the *Sultan*, 74; the *Superb*, 74; the *Monarca*, 74; the *Exeter*, 64; the *Sceptre*, 64; the *Eagle*, 64; the *Magnamine*, 64; the *Monmouth*, 64; the *Isis*, 56; the *Worcester*, 54; and five frigates and one corvette, carrying in all 976 guns.

4

or effectually disable, the fleet of Sir Edward Hughes, everything was still possible. Bussy was on the point of arriving; Haidar Ali still lived, threatening the English possessions all round Madras; the attenuated English army, deprived of its fleet, would be unable to keep the field; and there was nothing to prevent the victorious French fleet from sailing with the monsoon wind to Madras, and crushing out the domination of the English in the countries south of the river Krishna. There was the one obstacle offered by the twelve ships of Sir Edward Hughes; and Suffren had fourteen.

That Suffren entertained such hopes is beyond a doubt. Writing to a friend on the 14th, after the battle I am about to describe, and alluding to the excellent conduct of the captain of the *Illustre* M. de Bruyères de Chalabre, he used this expression: "No one could have "borne himself better than he did; if all had done like "him, we should have been masters of India for "ever."*

But let us now turn to the events of this memorable day. Decided by the signal from the *Bellona* to fight, Suffren, after a short exhortation to his captains, weighed anchor, and stood out towards the enemy who appeared inclined to entice him gently away from the harbour. As he approached, he signalled to form line in the prearranged order. This signal, though repeated again and again, was so badly executed by some of the

* This letter was published in the *Gazette de France* of 31st March, 1783.

malcontent captains, that it appeared to the English as if their enemy was about, after all, to decline an engagement. At length, however, their intentions became clear. Their line, though badly formed—the ships being at unequal distances from each other, here crowded, there separated by a long interval—approached till within cannonshot.

Suffren, dissatisfied with the unequal formation his ships had taken up, signalled then to his captains to reserve their fire till they should be at close quarters with the enemy. He endeavoured to enforce this order by firing a gun. The signal was misunderstood to signify the immediate opening of fire. The fire accordingly opened simultaneously along the whole line of the fleet. The compliment was quickly returned, and in a few minutes the action became general.

Leaving for a moment the van and rear guards of both fleets, we will turn our attention to the centre, in which the rival commanders were opposed to each other. The French centre was composed of the *Héros*, the *Illustre*, the *Sphinx*, the *Flamand*, and the *Petit Annibal*. Of these five the *Sphinx* and the *Petit Annibal* had, by bad seamanship or ill-will on the part of their captains, mixed themselves with the vanguard, the *Flamand* had tacked herself on the rearguard, whilst, on the other hand, the *Ajax*, of the rearguard, had joined the centre. It was then, with only three vessels, the *Héros*, the *Illustre*, and the *Ajax*, that Suffren came to close quarters with the English admiral.

Here he found ready to receive him, and arranged with that care for discipline and obedience to orders which is one of the glories of the English services, the *Burford*, the *Superb*, the *Sultan*, the *Eagle*, the *Hero*, and the *Monarca*. For one hour the unequal combat lasted, fought with admirable courage on both sides; at the end of that period Suffren saw that the odds were too great, and that, unless he received prompt assistance, he must succumb. He signalled, therefore, to the *St. Michel*, commanded by d'Aymar, and to the *Annibal*, commanded by de Tromelin, to come to his aid. Neither obeyed. De Kersaison, however, brought up the *Brillant*, though not in a position to offer the most effectual assistance.

Whilst this murderous hand-to-hand conflict was going on in the centre, the two extremities continued pounding at each other at long distances. In this the French had somewhat the advantage. The *Exeter* was disabled, and forced to draw out of the line; the *Isis* suffered severely, and her captain, Lumley, was killed; the *Worcester*, who lost her captain, Wood, and the *Monmouth*, were riddled. On the French side, the *Consolante*, a 40-gun frigate, which had been brought into action, lost her captain, Péan; the *Vengeur*, having fired away all her ammunition, withdrew from the line, and caught fire, with difficulty extinguished; the remainder of the squadron continued to fire without order, and at long distances, notwithstanding that the signal for close action was still flying on the commodore's ship.

At four o'clock in the afternoon, the fight having lasted then one hour and a half, the situation of the French commodore had become extremely critical. The *Ajax* had been so riddled as to be able to retire only with the greatest difficulty. The *Héros*, the *Illustre*, and the *Brillant* had to bear unsupported the weight of the concentrated fire of the centre division of the English fleet. At four o'clock the *Artésien* came to the commodore's rescue; but even then the odds were too great. About five o'clock the mainmast, the fore topmast, and the mizen topmast of the *Héros* came down with a tremendous crash. The hurrahs of the English first showed Suffren that they thought he had struck his flag. Not for long did they remain under this delusion. Rushing on the poop, Suffren cried with a voice that sounded above the roar of the combat: "Bring flags; " bring up all the white flags that are below and cover my " ship with them." These words inspired his men with renewed energy. The contest continued with greater fury than ever. The *Burford*, the *Sultan*, and the *Superb* had already felt, and now felt again its effects. Hope was beginning to rise, when at the moment it was whispered to Suffren that he had already expended 1800 rounds of shot, and that his ammunition was exhausted!

Powder, however, remained, and with powder alone he continued the fire, so as to delude the enemy. But he had begun to despair; already he was thinking of spiking the guns, and, enticing the enemy's ships close to him, of blowing up his ship and her neighbours with her, when an event occurred which changed the fortunes of the day.

Suddenly, at half-past five, the wind shifted from the south-west to the east-south-east. This enabled the vanguard of the French fleet to come to the aid of, and to cover, its centre. At the same time the English fleet wore. But on resuming its position it had no longer the hardly-pressed ships of the French centre to encounter, but those of the vanguard which till then had only engaged at a distance and were comparatively fresh.

The battle then re-engaged. But now it was the turn of the French. The *Hero* lost her mainmast at twenty minutes past six and her mizenmast soon after. The maintopmast of the *Worcester* was shot away about the same time. The *Superb*, the *Burford*, the *Eagle*, and the *Monmouth* had previously been disabled.

At length night fell, and the engagement ceased—another drawn battle. Both fleets remained all night near the scene of action. The next morning that of the French entered the harbour of Trincomali, the English set sail for Madras.*

* It is very difficult to reconcile the accounts given by the rival actors of the latter part of the action. The English writers assert that the French entered the harbour that very night. Vice-Admiral Bouët-Willaumez and the French authorities of the time assert that Suffren signalled to chase the English, but that they got away; and that the French entered Trincomali the next morning. Truth would appear to be that both sides were thoroughly exhausted, and were glad to discontinue the battle; that both anchored that night near to where they had fought, and that the French entered the harbour early in the morning.

Such was the great sea fight off Trincomali. That the majority of the French captains behaved disgracefully was broadly asserted by Suffren, and was admitted by his adversaries. In the English accounts published in India at that period those captains were stigmatised as being "unworthy to serve so great a man," whilst even in the *Calcutta Gazette* it was admitted that Suffren had been very badly seconded. There can scarcely be a doubt that he was right in saying as he did in the letter I have already referred to, that if all had fought like the captain of the *Illustre* he would have mastered Southern India. As it was, the battle was not without his effect on the campaign.

The Madras Government was so sensible of the damages sustained by the English fleet, and so cognizant of the enterprising spirit of the French commodore, that they ordered their army to fall back on Madras. Had there been at the head of the French land forces a man possessing but the atom of a brain, the dream of Dupleix, of Lally, and of Suffren, might even then have been realised!

The consequences to some of the French captains were serious. On the 13th September de Tromelin of the *Annibal*, de St. Félix of the *Artésien*, and de la Landelle of the *Bizarre*, were shipped off the Isle of France. They were accompanied by de Galles of the *Petit Annibal*, whose health rendered necessary the change.

The French fleet having repaired damages, and

having lost one of its vessels (*l'Orient*), which struck on a rock the morning after the action, sailed from Trincomali on the 30th September, and arrived off Kadalúr on the 4th October. Here Suffren had the misfortune to lose the *Bizarre* which, taken too near the shore, ran aground. On the 15th, he set out with the remainder of his ships to winter at Achin. He arrived there on the 7th November.

It is time now to take a glance at the land operations.

V.

We left the French auxiliary land force under Duchemin in the strongly fortified position of Kalinúr,—a position in which Haidar Ali had left them in disgust at the conduct of their commander, to go in person with his own troops alone to baffle the designs of Coote on Arni (2nd June, 1782). We have seen how he accomplished that task. Shortly after the action which took place before that fortress, and the more trifling skirmishes that followed, the English army retired to the vicinity of Madras.

On his side Haidar Ali cantoned his main army on the high ground near the river Poni, sixteen miles north of Arcot, conducting thence the siege of Vellor. Thence also he despatched his son Tippú, with a considerable force, to counteract the manœuvres of the English on the western coast. The French auxiliary force under Duchemin remained intrenched near Kadalúr in a state of complete inactivity. Here on the 13th September Duchemin, who had been long ailing, died. He was succeeded by Count d'Offelize, the colonel of the regiment of Austrasia, a man respected for his judgment and good sense.

But it was soon seen that active hostilities had by no means ceased. Taking advantage of the absence of Haidar at Kadalúr, whither he had repaired for his interview with the French commodore, Sir Eyre Coote had succeeded by a sudden and rapid march, in introducing a six month's supply of stores and ammunition into the threatened fortress of Vellor. Haidar, who had too late received intelligence of his enemy's movement, hastened to attempt to defeat it, but arrived only in time to witness its successful execution. Haidar then returned to his camp on the river Poni. Coote, waiting until the excitement caused by his recent raid should have subsided, thought it might just be possible to steal a march upon the ruler of Mysore, and, pouncing upon Kadalúr, not only to seize that fortified depôt, but to destroy at a blow the French auxiliary force. He had every hope that in this attempt he would be supported by the frigate and transports containing stores and a battering train, which had been expedited from Madras for that purpose. He therefore attempted it.

Succeeding in eluding the vigilance of Haidar, Coote found himself, on the 6th September, on the red hills near Pondichery. He commanded thence a complete view of the sea. But to his disappointment not a sail was to be seen. There was but a march between him and the French encampment. Without a battering train, however, the chances of success were slight, and repulse would be fatal, for Haidar would not long delay to act on his communications. As it was, even, his position was full of peril. Still he maintained it for some days, straining his eyes towards the sea. Nor did he cease to hope, until an express from Madras informed him that Trincomali had fallen into the hands of the enemy, and that the fleet, badly treated in an encounter before that place, was in full sail for Madras. He at once resigned hope and fell back on the presidency town.

Seldom, it may be safely affirmed, have English interests in Southern India been exposed to greater danger than they were on this occasion. Haidar was encamped in an impregnable position within easy distance of Madras; two thousand of the famed horsemen of Mysore encircled the capital endeavouring to cut off supplies; a large addition to the French land force was momentarily expected; the fleet, by the capture of Trincomali, had been deprived of the only possible place of refuge on the Coromandel coast during the N.E. monsoon, then about to break: and, added to all, a famine, such as had not been known for years, was devastating the country.* It seemed that it required

* A contemporary, the author of *Transactions in India*, writing three years after the event, thus describes the famine and its consequences: "At this moment a famine raged in Madras and every part of the Carnatic, and by the tempest now described, all foreign resources that depended on an intercourse by sea were at an end. * * * The roads, the outlets and even the streets (of Madras) were everywhere choked up with heaps of dead and crowds of the dying. Two hundred at least of the natives perished every day in the streets and the suburbs. * * * All was done which private charity could do; but it was a whole people in beggary; a nation which stretched out its hand for food. * * * For eighteen months did this destruction rage from the gates of Madras to the gates of Tanjor."

but one energetic push on the part of the enemy to make the whole edifice of British supremacy topple over.

The damages sustained by the English ships in the action off Trincomali rendered it dangerous for them to wait the first burst of the monsoon in the open roadstead of Madras. Sir Edward Hughes, therefore, immediately after his arrival, announced to the Governor, Lord Macartney, his intention to take his fleet round to Bombay as soon as he should be able to patch up the injured ships. In vain did the Governor remonstrate. Sir Edward Hughes was obdurate, and rightly obdurate. He knew well the force of the monsoon and his inability to brave it. He therefore adhered to his resolution.

His efforts to put his ships in order, to re-victual and re-equip them, were stimulated not less by the close proximity of the monsoon, than by a report which reached Madras that Suffren was about to make an attempt on Negapatam.* With all his efforts, however, Hughes could not sail before the 15th October; but on the 15th October he sailed.

The morning of the 15th had been threatening, showing every indications of a storm. The result did not belie the promise. The following morning the long line of coast off Madras was strewed with wrecks; many vessels foundered, some were driven on shore. Of the small craft containing the rice supplies which had been sent from the more northern ports and roadsteads, not a single one remained.

* He had been seen off Negapatam on the 1st October.

The ships of Sir Edward Hughes though they escaped absolute destruction met with little short of it. For a whole month no two ships of the fleet could speak with each other. The *Superb*, which carried the admiral's flag, had been at an early date reduced to such a condition that Sir Edward took the first opportunity to shift his flag to the *Sultan*. They were upwards of two months in making the voyage to Bombay. And when the admiral arrived there on the 20th December, he arrived with a shattered fleet and with sickly crews.*

Four days after the departure of Sir Edward Hughes from Madras, Sir Robert Bickerton arrived there with five ships of war and a large number of transports having on board about 4000 infantry and 340 cavalry. Having landed these he, too, sailed for Bombay.

Meanwhile Suffren had arrived at Achin (7th November). He stayed there till the 15th January, engaged in refitting his ships, in attending to his crews, and in sending cruisers into the Bay of Bengal, where they made some important captures.† Early in January he heard of the death of Haidar Ali (7th December.) He determined therefore to return at once to the

* It is a curious circumstance connected with the law of storms, first that Suffren, who left Kadalúr the same day as that on which Sir E. Hughes left Madras, experienced only fine weather. He noticed the coming storm and avoided it; that Sir R. Bickerton reached Madras with five sail of the line on the 19th October without experiencing bad weather; that he left it, the very day he had landed his troops, for Bombay, and arrived there some weeks before Sir E. Hughes without experiencing any bad weather in transit.

† Amongst others the *Coventry*, a frigate carrying 32 guns.

Coromandel coast to concert fresh measures with Tippú Sultan.

Suffren, sailing on the 15th January, arrived off Kadalúr early in February. He was surprised to find there neither tidings of Bussy, nor any news regarding two ships of his fleet, the *Annibal* and *Bellona*, which he had sent to cruise in the Bay of Bengal. He stayed there but a few days; then, having detached two of his ships, the *St. Michel* and the *Coventry*, towards Madras to intercept an English convoy, he sailed for Trincomali, and arrived there on the 23rd February.

Here he was joined not only by his missing ships, but, on the 10th March, by the squadron which was escorting Bussy, consisting of three line of battle ships, one frigate and thirty-two transports.

The troops under the command of the Marquis de Bussy, consisting of about 2300 men,* were escorted to the Coromandel coast and were landed safely at Porto Novo on the 19th March. I propose now to show the state in which the new commander found the affairs of the French and their ally.

The English having concluded peace with the Márhátás had, early in the year, made in communication with them so strong a demonstration on the western coast, that Tippú had been forced to start with the bulk of his army to defend his own dominions. But

* They consisted of detachments from the regiment de la Mark, from the regiment d'Aquitaine, from the Royal Roussillon, and of 300 artillery men.

before this had happened General Stuart had succeeded Sir Eyre Coote in command of the English forces at Madras. Reinforced, as we have seen, Stuart moved in February on to Karangúli and Wandewash, the fortifications of which places he destroyed. The Mysorean army under Tippú and the French auxiliaries under d'Offelize were occupying a position at the time within twelve miles of Wandewash, and an action between their army and the English seemed at one time imminent; but Tippú's preparations had not been completed when Stuart offered battle, and when Tippú's plans had matured Stuart had retired. It was immediately after this that Tippú started with the bulk of his army and one French regiment for Mysore, leaving 3000 infantry and 7000 cavalry at the disposal of d'Offelize.

The English authorities still clung to the plan of wresting, by a combined attack by sea and land, the fortified depôt of Kadalúr from the French. Arrangements having been concerted with Sir Edward Hughes, Stuart set out from the vicinity of Madras on the 21st April, at the head of about 15,000 men.* As he advanced to Wandewash, d'Offelize, whose European force had been reduced to about 600 men, fell back in the direction of Kadalúr.

Bussy, we have seen, arrived at Kadalúr on the 19th March, in plenty of time, by an active initiative, to prevent the investiture of that place. But the Bussy who

* He set out with about 3000 Europeans and 11,500 natives, but was joined almost immediately by 600 Europeans just landed.

returned to India in 1783 was no longer the hardy warrior who had electrified Southern India in the years between 1754 and 1760; who had made of the Subadar of the Dekhan a French prefect, and whose capacity to dare had supplied the want of soldiers. If the Bussy of 1756, by his genius, his activity, his daring, his success, foreshadowed in some respects the illustrious warrior who, just forty years later, displayed the same qualities to conquer Italy, the Bussy of 1783, corrupted by wealth, enervated by luxury, and careful only of his ease, more resembled that scion of the House of Bourbon, once his sovereign, who consecrated all his hours to his mistresses, who left the nomination of the generals of the armies of France to a de Pompadour, and who banished a Choiseul on the requisition of a Du Barry!

Bussy, then, instead of acting with vigour, did nothing. He did not even show himself to his men. He kept himself—to borrow the language of one of his countrymen—" invisible in his tent like a rich Nabob." Instructed by Colonel d'Offelize of the advance of the English, and informed by that officer that he pledged himself to maintain his force at Permacól, if he were but supported, Bussy not only refused, but abandoned every outlying fortification and fell back within Kadalúr.

The fort of Kadalúr was a quadrangle of unequal sides, extremely weak in many respects, and possessing an indifferent flanking defence. From two to four miles from its western face inland were the hills of Bandapalam. A little estuary formed by the sea covered the eastern and southern faces. It was defended by the whole French force, reduced now, by sickness and detachments lent to Tippú, to 2300 Europeans, and by a Mysorean force of 3000 infantry and 7000 horse.

The English army arrived before Kadalúr on the 4th June. On the 7th, secure of the support of the fleet, which had arrived at Porto Novo, it made a circuit round the hill and took up a position two miles southward from the fort, its left resting on the hills, its right on the estuary. In making this circuit, Stuart so exposed his left to the enemy, that the major of the regiment of Austrasia, de Boisseaux, ventured to disturb the "French "Nabob" in his tent, to point out the capital crime the English were committing. But Bussy, not with difficulty, restrained himself. He had arrived at a time of life when men no longer attack.

It was only when Stuart had definitely taken up his position to the south that Bussy formed up his force outside Kadalúr, in a line nearly parallel to the enemy, and began to cover it with intrenchments.

On the 13th General Stuart ordered an attack on the right of the French line under the command of Colonel Kelly. The attack, after gaining two positions, was, thanks to the skill and energy of Colonel d'Offelize, repulsed with great loss at the third. The success of the French seemed assured, but they pursued the retiring enemy too far, and General Stuart, noticing his opportunity came up between them and their intrenchments, and gained a position which would enable him, as soon as his battering train, then on board the fleet, should be landed, to command the entire French line of defence. Upon this the fight ceased, and Bussy, who for the day had exchanged his tent for a palanquin, withdrew his troops during the night within Kadalúr.

All this time the sea had been commanded by the English fleet. But on the evening of the day on which the French had been driven within Kadalúr, a circumstance occurred which brings again upon the scene the illustrious French admiral* at the hour of the direst needs of his country.

We left Suffren on the 19th March landing the army of Bussy at Porto Novo. Coasting then southwards, he arrived on the 11th April, after a slow and difficult journey, within sight of Trincomali. In spite of the presence of the English off the coast he entered the harbour, and at once set to work to refit his fleet. Of his fifteen ships all but five were still under repair, when, on the 24th May, the English fleet again passed Trincomali in full sail to the south. Imagining that this demonstration was but a feint to draw him towards Kadalúr so that Trincomali might be captured in his absence, Suffren contented himself with sending some transports escorted by frigates to Kadalúr, and continued his repairs. Again, on the 31st May, the English fleet appeared, bearing northwards, and this time it even made a demonstration to attack the harbour. But it was only

* Suffren had been promoted in March, 1783, to the rank of *lieutenant-général*, a title corresponding to that of vice-admiral.

a demonstration. At the end of two days Sir Edward Hughes went on to take up at Porto Novo a position which was to support the attack of the land army on Kadalúr. Two days later the French frigates and transports which had been sent to convey stores to Kadalúr returned to Trincomali. The senior captain of the expedition brought with him a letter from Bussy, written early in June, painting his needs and imploring assistance.

Suffren was not the man to turn a deaf ear to an exhortation of that nature. It is true that he knew his fleet to be inferior in number, in condition, and in weight of metal to that of the enemy;* but he felt that the interests of France would be better served by his provoking an unequal contest, the issue of which might however be favourable, than by allowing her last army to succumb without a blow.† He therefore did not hesitate for a moment. He did not even consult any one; but summoning on board the flagship the captains of his fleet, he informed them in a few spirit-stirring words that the army at Kadalúr was lost unless the fleet went to succour it; and that the glory of saving it was reserved for them; and that, whatever might be the result, they would at least attempt it.

These words were received by the assembled captains with the greatest enthusiasm. Instantly every hand

* The French fleet consisted of fifteen ships of war and one frigate carrying 1008 guns; the English of eighteen ships of war, carrying, 1202 guns.

† The conduct of Suffren on this occasion may well be contrasted with that of d'Ache in 1761.—*Vide History of the French in India.*

lent itself to the work. The crews of all but three of the frigates were transferred to the line of battle ships to bring up the complement of these to working capacity. On the 11th June the fleet left Trincomali. On the evening of the 13th it came within sight of Kadalúr to gladden by its appearance the hearts of the soldiers who had been forced that day to retire within its fortifications.

Sir Edward Hughes was at Porto Novo. His light ships having signalled the French fleet, he at once stood in for Kadalúr, and anchored in front of it. The 14th and 15th, the state of the wind rendered it impossible for Suffren to force on an action, and the English admiral, rightly regarding the capture of Kadalúr as the main object of the campaign, conceived that he best contributed to the accomplishment of that object by covering the besieged fort. On the 16th, however, the wind changed, and the French fleet bore down on its enemy. The English admiral at once weighed anchor and stood to sea, hoping that by standing out and catching the light breezes which he thought he detected in the open, he might bear down in his turn and take Suffren at disadvantage. But this did not happen, and Suffren, still bearing towards the coast, reaped the fruit of his happy audacity by occupying, without firing a shot, the place in front of Kadalúr which had just been vacated by his English rival!

It is impossible to speak in terms of too high commendation of this display of combined genius and daring. To beat on the open sea a fleet of equal or of greater numbers is no doubt a splendid achievement; but it is an achievement in which the lower nature of man, that which is termed brute force, has a considerable share. But to gain all the effect of a victory without fighting, to dislodge an enemy superior in numbers from a position of vital importance without firing a shot—that indeed is an exercise of the highest faculties of man's higher nature, a feat of intellectual power not often bestowed, but generally combined, when given, with that strength of nerve which knows when and how to dare.*

The clocks of Kadalúr were striking half-past eight when Suffren anchored before the town. With the prescience of a true commander he had discovered that of the two enemies before him it was necessary to drive off the one before attacking the other. Were he to lend his sailors to join in an attack on General Stuart, he might at any moment be assailed at a disadvantage

* It is curious to note the manner in which this achievement is alluded to by English writers. Wilks, with his usual straightforwardness, writes thus: "On the 16th, he (Hughes) weighed anchor, with the expectation of bringing the enemy to close action, but such was the superior skill or fortune of M. Suffren that on the same night, at half-past eight, he anchored abreast of the fort, and the dawn of day presented to the English army before Cuddalore the mortifying spectacle of the French fleet in the exact position abandoned by their own on the previous day, the English fleet being invisible and its situation unknown." The author of *Memoirs of the late War in Asia*, himself a combatant, speaks of the French fleet as "a crazy fleet, consisting of fifteen sail of ships, half of them in very bad condition." He merely mentions that "it occupied the place vacated by Sir E. Hughes' fleet, consisting of eighteen coppered ships (their crews greatly debilitated by sickness)." Campbell and the writer of the *Transactions* pass over the event in silence. Even Mill ignores it; but it is a well-attested fact.

by Admiral Hughes. Instead therefore of disembarking his own men he embarked 1000 soldiers to strengthen his ships.

This embarkation took place on the 17th. On the 18th Suffren weighed anchor and stood out, but neither on that day nor on the day following could he succeed in bringing the enemy to action. On the 20th Sir Edward Hughes, whose men were suffering from scurvy, and whose supplies of water were running short,* found it absolutely necessary to accept a contest or to bear up for Madras. He chose the former alternative.

In the contest which was about to commence Suffren was in number of ships, in their condition, and in weight of metal considerably inferior to the English.† On the other hand his ships were better manned. But that which gave him the greatest confidence was the

* He had lost, during little more than a month, nearly 3000 men from the same cause. It is to this that the English writers attribute his unwillingness to accept an engagement.

† The English fleet consisted of the *Gibraltar*, 80, the *Defence*, 74, the *Hero*, 74, the *Sultan*, 74, the *Superb*, 74, the *Cumberland*, 74, the *Monarca*, 70, the *Burford*, 70, the *Inflexible*, 64, the *Exeter*, 64, the *Worcester*, 64, the *Africa*, 64, the *Sceptre*, 64, the *Magnamine*, 64, the *Eagle*, 64, the *Monmouth*, 64, the *Bristol*, 50, the *Isis*, 50.

The French fleet, of the *Fendant*, 74, the *Argonaute*, 74, the *Héros*, 74, the *Illustre*, 74, the *Annibal*, 74, the *Sphinx*, 64, the *Brillant*, 64, the *Ajax*, 64, the *Vengeur*, 64, the *Sévère*, 64, the *Hardi*, 64, the *Artésien*, 64, the *St. Michel*, 60, the *Flamand*, 50, the *Petit Annibal*, 50, and the *Consolante* frigate, 40, brought into the line. The French had also three frigates, the *Fine*, the *Cléopâtre*, and the *Coventry*. On board of one of these, in consequence of an express order of the king, provoked by the capture of Count de Grasse in his contest with Rodney, Suffren hoisted his flag during the action. The English had also two frigates, the *Active* and the *Medea*.

quality of his captains. For the first time the ships of his fleet were commanded by men whom he could trust.

At quarter-past four in the afternoon, the two fleets, having come within range, almost simultaneously opened fire. Immediately afterwards the *Flamand*, 50, attempting to pierce the enemy's line, was attacked on both sides by the *Exeter* and the *Inflexible*. Her captain, de Salvart, was killed, but the first lieütenant succeeded in rescuing her from her perilous position.

Whilst this was being attempted the *Héros* and *Illustre* engaged at once the *Superb*, the *Monarca* and the *Burford;* the *Argonaute* the *Sultan;* the *Petit Annibal* the *Africa;* the *Vengeur* the *Magnamine;* the *Hardi* at once the *Bristol* and the *Monmouth*. In the rear division the *Fendant* encountered first the *Inflexible* and then the *Gibraltar*, whilst the *Sphinx* tackled the *Defence*. The other ships of both fleets were not less actively engaged.

At about half-past five the mizen topmast of the *Fendant* caught fire, and her commander was forced to take her for a moment out of the line. The *Gibraltar*, with whom she had been engaged, seized this opportunity to attempt to break the French line, but the *Flamand* covered her consort and kept the enemy at bay till the fire was extinguished, and the *Fendant* returned to her position.

The murderous contest was kept up on both sides until past seven o'clock, when darkness supervened and the firing ceased. Neither fleet had lost a ship, both had been severely handled; but the practical victory would be naturally to that which would be able to compel the other to retire from the vicinity of Kadalúr. That question was soon decided.

During the night the French fleet beat about endeavouring to remain close to Kadalúr, but the currents took it down to Pondichery. There, in the course of of the following day, it anchored but early on the morning of the 22nd, his light ships signalling the English fleet bearing N.N.E., Suffren immediately weighed anchor and stood out in pursuit. When, however, he reached Kadalúr the enemy was no longer in sight; Sir E. Hughes had borne up for Madras.*

Thus then had Suffren by combined skill and valour attained one of his objects. He had driven one enemy from the coast; he would now aid in forcing the other to retreat. That same evening, the 23rd June, he landed not only the 1000 soldiers he had borrowed from the fort, but added to them 2400 men from his sailors.

More he could not do. He could command and win

* The impartial historian, Lieutenant-Colonel Wilks, by no means a lover of the French, states that "The English Admiral, after receiving the detailed reports of the state of each ship, found the whole of his equipments so entirely crippled, his crews so lamentably reduced, and the want to water so extreme, that he deemed if indispensable to incur the mortification of bearing away for the roads of Madras whilst Suffren, wresting from his enemies the praise of superior address and *even the claim of victory, if victory belong to him who attains his object*, resumed his position in the anchorage of Cuddalore." The italics are my own. Campbell and the author of the *Transactions* are, as usual, vague when the matter refers to the success of the French.

battles on sea. He could send his men on shore, but on land his own men, he himself even, came under the orders of Bussy. And we have seen what the Bussy of 1783 was. Yet this man, once so distinguished, had now an opportunity at the like of which he would have clutched in his younger days. Covered by the fleet, he could make an assault on the enemy—the landing of whose battering train had been prevented by the success of Suffren—with numbers superior to their own. Suffren urged him to this course; d'Offelize urged him; the officers of his staff urged him. But he would not. He let the golden moments slip. Then Suffren, disgusted, returned on board his ship, asking Bussy as he left him "if he expected that he could take his ships to "beat the enemy on shore."

At last, after many hesitations, when General Stuart had recovered from the moral depression which the departure of the English fleet and, with it, his battering train, had caused him, Bussy determined to risk a sortie. But a sortie to succeed must be composed of picked men, and those men must be well commanded. Bussy neglected both these necessary precautions. The men he ordered for the work were not only not specially selected, but their number was insufficient for the purpose; their leader moreover, the Chevalier de Dumas, was the least trusted officer in the French force.* The result corresponded to the plan.

* C'était un vil intrigant d'une incapacité reconnue.—*Roux.* Wilks says he was inconsolable at not having been wounded.

The sortie, made at three o'clock in the morning of the 26th June, was repulsed with the loss of about forty men killed, and 100 taken prisoners.*

Notwithstanding this repulse, the English general was too well aware of his own comparative weakness to attempt an assault. He restricted himself therefore to a blockade, and that of merely a nominal nature. The French troops drew in unopposed all their supplies from the country, and Bussy—even the Bussy of 1783—had become so emboldened as to talk of an attack on the besiegers' camp with his combined force, when suddenly the intelligence that the preliminaries of peace had been signed in Europe, induced both contending parties to agree to a suspension of arms.

This suspension assumed on the 3rd September following a permanent character, by the announcement of the conclusion of the peace known in history as the treaty of Versailles.

The suspension of arms was most unfortunate for France. The army of Stuart before Kadalúr represented the last hope of the English in Southern India. It was reduced then by the want of supplies to the greatest extremities. An attack by the French in force could

* Amongst the prisoners taken was Bernadotte, afterwards Marshal of France, Prince of Pontecorvo, and King of Sweden. He was then a sergeant in the regiment of Aquitaine. After he had attained greatness Bernadotte seized the earliest opportunity of expressing to Colonel Langenheim, who commanded the German legion at Kadalúr, and whom he met again in Hanover, his sense of the kindness with which he had been treated on this occasion.

have scarcely failed to annihilate it. With its destruction Madras and all Southern India would have passed over to the French.*

But it was not to be; nor, even if it had been, can it be imagined that the scion of the House of Bourbon who then governed France, well-intentioned though he may have been, would have refused to restore it without conditions. His predecessor, after having lavished French blood and spent French treasure in a war which was costly, and in spite of himself successful, restored at the peace which followed † all his conquests, and agreed even to dismiss his guest from his hearth, saying he "would not treat as a tradesman but as a king." This kingly method of benefiting one's adversaries at the expense of one's country would seem to be an heirloom of the House of Bourbon. For, with respect to India, the treaty of Versailles carried out precisely the same principle. The war which that treaty terminated had been a most disastrous war for England. She had lost, and rightly lost, her American colonies; she seemed, for the moment, shorn of her prestige; the French could have insisted at least on the restoration of her possessions in India to the *status quo ante* 1761. This was a cardinal point which neither the Republic

* Professor H. H. Wilson thus writes on this subject: "It seems probable that but for the opportune occurrence of peace with France, the South of India would have been lost to the English. The annihilation of the army at Cuddalore would have been followed by the siege of Madras, and there was little chance of defending it successfully against Tippoo and the French."

† The Peace of Aix la Chapelle.

nor the Empire would have foregone. But the Bourbons "treated as kings and not as traders." Consequently, though England had but one army in Southern India, and that army was exposed to destruction, Louis XVI. renounced every advantage, and allowed French India to accept, after a victorious campaign, conditions almost identical with those which had been forced upon her after the capture of her capital in 1761.

Yet the indifference of the ruler of France, noxious as it was to French interests, could not detract in the smallest degree from the merits of the illustrious man who did, for a time, restore French influence to Southern India. That man was the Bailli* de Suffren. His five contests with an English fleet, of always nearly equal, once even of greater force, stamp him as being inferior to none of the great seamen whom France and England had till then produced. This has been virtually admitted by the writers on naval subjects of both nations. Mr. Clerk, whose work on naval tactics, originally published in 1778, is said to have inspired Rodney with the famous idea of breaking the line, republished, in 1790, an edition in which he cites the manœuvres of Suffren as constituting a lesson to all admirals to come, and indicates him as having been the first commander to introduce the principle of fighting at close quarters, subsequently carried to so great a perfection by Nelson. Vice-Admiral Bouët Willaumez, in his work entitled

* In 1782 he had been nominated Bailli of the order of the Knights of St. John of Jerusalem.

Batailles de terre et de mer, says of Suffren that he was "the first to disdain the routine professed by the "admirals of his epoch, consisting of ranging the "squadron in one single line of battle. He cared not "for the traditions which required one to fight at a "moderate distance. He engaged within pistol-shot." The naval historian, Dr. Campbell, whose anti-French sympathies are so strongly marked, is forced to admit that Suffren was "worthy of being the rival and "opponent of Sir Edward Hughes." I have already cited the opinion of Colonel Wilks. Amongst all the works I have consulted on the subject I have not found a divergent sentiment.

The character of Suffren is thus justly summarised by M. Hennequin,* "To an imperturbable coolness in "action, Suffren united an extreme ardour and activity. "Couràgeous even to rashness, he showed an inflexible "rigour towards officers whom he suspected of weakness "or cowardice. In a word, he united in his person all "the qualities which make a warrior illustrious, a sailor "skilful, and a man esteemed. Those who knew him, "and especially the officers who sailed under his orders, "never pronounce his name even now but with respect "and admiration."

Suffren returned to France in 1784, to receive high honours from his Sovereign, but he did not long survive to enjoy them. He was killed in a duel in 1788 at the age of sixty-two.

* *Essai historique sur la vie et les campagnes du Bailli de Suffren.*

Had he but lived, would he have been too old to command the fleet which fought Lord Howe on the 1st June, 1794? Could he have occupied with advantage the place of Brueys and Villeneuve? These are questions which the French at least, who owned him and who glory in him, do ask, and which they have a right to ask. Nor will we—we English—who honour genius, and who recognise that genius in the man who, though a foreigner, was still the precursor of our own Nelson, grudge them the answer which their pride and their patriotism alike dictate.

Meanwhile peace between the European rivals reigned again in Southern India. By the interval of nine years which elapsed between the signature of the treaty of Versailles and the outbreak of the war of the Revolution the English profited to fix their domination on a basis so substantial as to be proof against further direct hostility on the part of their great rival. But the indirect efforts which were then attempted were coloured by a tinge of romance almost entirely wanting in the history I have just recorded.

BOOK II.

THE ISLE OF FRANCE AND HER PRIVATEERS.

I.

Between the peace of Versailles and the outbreak of the Revolutionary war, the French Marine was but thinly represented on the Indian seas. But when in 1793, war was declared between the two nations, the flag of the French Republic, that flag which so soon was 'to make the tour of Europe,' appeared again to animate those whom it represented to fight, not on this occasion for victory, but for existence.

For, indeed, at the outset of the struggle the navy of France was far from being in a condition to combat the ships of her ancient rival with any prospect of success. The nobility, from which its officers had been drawn, had emigrated in large numbers, and the democratic principle, which had been introduced upon the ruins of that which had crumbled away because its foundations had rotted, had been denied the opportunity granted to the land forces of developing, on the spur of the moment, a perfect system of promotion and command. Nevertheless, even under these trying circumstances, the navy of France proved not unworthy of the renown it had inherited from Tourville, from Duguay-Trouin, from Jean Bart, from de Forbin,* and from Suffren. The battle of the 1st June, fought by an untried admiral, with a fleet in no way superior to its enemy in numbers and weight of metal, and newly officered from the lowest to the highest grade,† was indeed a defeat, though not a very decisive defeat; yet who will say that under all the circumstances of the case, that defeat even was not glorious to the French arms?

Another cause which tended at this period to the

* The memoirs of the Count de Forbin, Commodore of the French Navy in the time of Louis XIV, were considered so remarkable that they were translated into English and published in London in the year 1731.

† Rear Admiral Kerguelen, writing at the time, gives an animated description of the flagrant mode in which officers were appointed to the ships of war "by charlatans and ignorant empirics." He gives details to prove his statements. Captain Brenton, R.N., writing on the same subject, says: "The French fleet was no longer manned and officered as in the splendid times of Louis XIV. * * Most of the seamen had been marched to the Rhine and the Moselle to fill the ranks of the army, and their places were supplied by wretched conscripts and fishermen. The captains of the line were men totally unqualified from their habits for such a station; they had been, with few exceptions, masters of merchantmen, and knew nothing of the signal book or of the mode of conducting a ship of war."

demoralisation and injury of the French fleet was the intense party-feeling which prevailed throughout the country. It was this party-feeling that induced Toulon, one of the great harbours of France, to revolt against the established form of government of the country. This revolt caused the loss to the French of twenty ships of the line and twenty-five frigates. Of these, three ships of the line, one of 120 guns, and twelve frigates, fell into the hands of the English — not conquered in fair fight, but betrayed by the partisans of the used-up race which France had expelled.

France, then, thus heavily weighted at starting, could dream no more of conquests on the Indian seas. She could not even defend her possessions on the mainland of India. These fell without a struggle to her fortunate rival. But she could still protect the islands, to the chief of which she had lent her own fair name; she could still protect her commerce; she could still inflict damage on the commerce of her enemy.* But to carry out this programme on the Indian waters, she had now

* That she was successful is shown by the following tables taken from the official documents :—

	Merchant Ships taken by the French from the English.	Merchant Ships taken by the English from the French.	
In 1793	261	63	Being a proportion in five years of more than six to one.
„ 1794	527	88	
„ 1795	502	47	
„ 1796	414	63	
„ 1797	562	114	
	2266	375	

no fleet available. To light squadrons, to single ships, to privateers, she had to leave these arduous duties. The deeds which were under such circumstances accomplished possess an interest all their own. Some of those performed by the privateers are worthy to be classed with the achievements of Duquesne, of Duguay-Trouin, and of Jean Bart.

Conspicuous amongst the commanders of these privateers was Robert Surcouf. His exploits were so intimately connected with the Indian seas; he took so leading a part in the devastation of English commerce from the very outbreak of hostilities; that I make no apology for bringing him at once before my readers, as one of the most considerable and the most successful of the naval adventurers with whom our countrymen had to deal on the Indian waters.

The advantages offered by the Isles of France and Bourbon as a refuge for French cruisers, whence these could sally to commit depredations upon British commerce, induced the British authorities to despatch in the early part of 1794 a squadron to watch and blockade the islands. This squadron, originally intended to consist of four ships, was finally composed only of the *Centurion* 50, Captain Osborne, and the *Diomede* 44, Captain Smith.

The islands, in the first throes of the revolution, had been virtually abandoned to their own resources by the mother country, nor did the latter fully resume her protective control until after the events of 18 Brumaire.

In the meanwhile the chief men in the islands, military, naval, and commercial, had formed a sort of provisional administration. The first question to be solved was that of "how to live?" This was answered in the manner I have indicated above. A few stray frigates and considerable and increasing number of privateers were sent to prey on the English commerce. Their gains, as may well be imagined, were enormous; and from a portion of these gains the treasury of the colonies was replenished.

The alarm which spread in the islands when the news reached them of the arrival in their waters of two English ships of war to intercept their cruisers can easily be imagined. There were not wanting, however, bold men, who forbade their fellow-colonists to despair and who promised to sally forth and drive away the daring strangers. Prominent amongst these adventurous spirits was Jean-Marie Renaud, a captain in the navy of France, and commodore of the small squadron which found itself at the time at the islands. This squadron consisted only of the frigates *Cybèle*, 40, and *Prudente*, 36, the brig *Courier*, 14, and the privateer *Jean-Bart*.* Renaud called a council of war of their captains, and as they agreed with him that boldness was prudence, he took out his little squadron that same afternoon to attack the strangers. He found them, and bore down

* The English historian, James, speaks of the *Jean-Bart* as a 20-gun corvette. She may have carried 20 guns, though that would seem doubtful, but she was only a privateer.

upon them at half-past three o'clock on the third day (22nd October.) The combat which followed was obstinate, bloody, and, as it appeared at the moment, indecisive. The French lost more men than the English; Renaud was wounded; his flag captain, Flouet, was killed; the same fate befell the first lieutenant of the *Cybèle*. Yet, in spite of these losses, the French succeeded in their main object. The two English ships renounced the blockade and disappeared.

At this time Robert Surcouf was engaged in cruising between the Isle of France and the coast of Africa. Born at St. Malo on the 12th December 1773, descended by his mother from the illustrious Duguay-Trouin, he had been sent to sea at the age of thirteen. In 1790 he made a voyage to India in the *Aurora*. On the breaking out of the war with England he was transferred to the French navy and returned to France. Arriving, he left the navy and set out as captain of a slaver, *le Créole*, for Africa. Having landed on the islands the negroes he had obtained, he quitted for ever that service, and accepted, in September 1765, the command of a privateer of 180 tons burden, carrying four six-pounders, and a crew of thirty men. The name of the vessel was *la Modeste*, but Surcouf changed it to *l'Emilie*.

For some reason the Governor of the islands, M. de Malartic, declined on this occasion to give Surcouf a letter of marque. He granted him permission only to defend himself in the event of his being attacked. Surcouf's ostensible mission was to proceed to the

Seychelles islands and procure thence a supply of turtle for the colonists.

The *Emilie* was a very fine sailer, and Surcouf, glowing with the ardour and enterprise of his twenty years, was a bold and daring seaman. He was not quite the man to be content with procuring turtle for his fellow-citizens. However, he directed his course straight to the Seychelles, and cast anchor off one of the islands on the 13th September. Here he stayed several days employing himself in taking on board articles of native produce. Already he had nearly loaded his vessel, when on the afternoon of the 7th October, he discovered two large English ships bearing down upon him from the south-east-by-south.

To cut his cable, to thread the intricacies of the navigation of the Archipelago, and to gain the high seas, was an object to which he instantly bent his energies. It was a daring exploit, for the navigation of the Seychelles islands was but little known, and many ships had been lost there. But, again, daring was prudence. With every sail set he traversed the difficult passages, then, finding himself in the open sea, he directed his course eastward. Caught by the changing monsoon, when approaching Achin, he again altered his course, determined to fly before it. When the fury of the storm had moderated, Surcouf turned the head of the *Emilie* towards Pegu. Scarcely, however, had he doubled Cape Negrais when he found himself almost face to face with an English vessel.

This was a trading ship, the *Penguin*, laden with wood. Surcouf captures her, places a few of his men on board, and starts her off for the islands. He then turns and follows as nearly as he can the coast towards the Bay of Bengal. He meets, however, no craft upon which he can seize; till, suddenly, at daybreak on the 19th January, he finds himself close to two English ships, towed by a pilot brig, at one of the mouths of the Ganges.

Surcouf attacked and took the three ships. Then, finding that the pilot brig was more adapted to his purposes than the *Emilie*, he removes to her his guns and his crew, calling her the *Cartier*, and sends off the *Emilie* in charge of his two prizes to the islands.

Still cruising off the mouths of the river, Surcouf discovered, on the evening of the 28th January, a large three-masted vessel going out to sea. He at once made for her and captured her. She proved to be the *Diana*, having on board a large cargo of rice. He then started with his prize for the islands.

But fortune was not always to befriend him. The very morning after the capture of the *Diana* he sighted a large English ship bearing up for the coast of Orissa. This was the *Triton*, an Indiaman carrying 26 guns and a crew of 150 men. Surcouf let the *Diana* approach him so as to increase his own crew, which, by the addition thus obtained, reached the number of nineteen men, himself and the surgeon included. He then set sail towards the *Triton*, of whose force he was naturally ignorant. Finding that she sailed better than the *Cartier*, he hoisted the Union Jack. The *Triton*, recognising the *Cartier* as a pilot brig, hove to. As Surcouf approached her he became for the first time aware of her formidable armament and of the number of her crew. At first he hoped these latter might be lascars, and it was not till he arrived within cannon-shot that he discovered them to be all Europeans.

He was lost. What could his seventeen men and four guns effect against the 150 men and twenty-six 12-pounders of the enemy? And he was within cannon-shot! Destruction seemed inevitable. He could not flee, for the *Triton* had shown herself a better sailer. The smallest hesitation would betray him. What was he to do?

Once more boldness was prudence. Not for one moment did Surcouf relax his onward movement. He summoned his crew, pointed out to them the enemy's guns, and told them that the *Triton* must be either their their tomb or the cradle of their glory. The crew declared with enthusiasm that they would conquer or die. Surcouf at once sent his men below; then, keeping near him only the master, the officer of the watch, a sailor, and two or three lascars whom he had taken from his prizes, he came up rapidly to within half pistol-shot on the windward quarter of the *Triton*. Then, suddenly replacing the Union Jack by the Tricolor, he fired a broadside on the group of sailors on the Indiaman's deck. Terror and astonishment contended with each other amongst the assaulted English. Surcouf at once turned his ship's head to the wind, clambered on board the *Triton*, and took advantage of the confusion which prevailed there to send up six men into the shrouds of the mizen-mast, thence, supported by the fire of their comrades, to carry the poop. A desperate struggle then ensued. The *Cartier* is ranged alongside the *Triton;* every Frenchman gains the deck; the English, surprised, unarmed, are one by one driven below; gradually the hatches are closed up by their gratings; the port-ropes are cut, and Surcouf does everything in his power to keep the enemy below.

Many of the English had been killed at the first broadside. The remainder, recovering from their surprise, made a manful resistance. Their indignation is increased by the discovery made by some of them of the small number of their assailants. They attempt to blow up the quarter deck; but Surcouf, discovering their project, opens so heavy a fire upon them through the main hatchway that they are forced to desist. At last, finding their efforts useless, the crew surrender.

Such was the capture of the *Triton*—a very Triton caught by a minnow—a capture so marvellous that even the Indian journals of the day wrote of it as "an extra-" ordinary capture."* Undoubtedly it was an act of piracy, for Surcouf bore no commission to attack English vessels, yet the captain of the *Triton* was necessarily ignorant of this deficiency in the powers of his enemy.

* *Madras Courier*, 16th February, 1796.

He knew that France and England were at war, and he ought to have known that an enemy will always take advantage of any ruse to gain his ends; that stratagem is fair in war.

Leaving out of consideration for a moment the defect in Surcouf's commission, it must be admitted that his conduct in most dangerous circumstances showed wonderful self-possession, daring, and nerve. He was not then twenty-two. Had he known the force of the *Triton* neither he, nor any man in his senses, would under the circumstances have attempted to capture her. But finding himself suddenly in a position from which it was impossible to escape, except by the display of a surpassing audacity and the happiest presence of mind, he, on the moment, did display those qualities—and conquered.

After the capture had been effected, Surcouf, embarrassed by the number of his prisoners, who greatly exceeded his own crew, ransomed the *Diana* to her former captain for a bill for 30,000 *sicca* rupees,* and after transferring to her his prisoners he let her go. Then, removing the bulk of his crew to the *Triton*, he sailed in her for the islands, instructing the *Cartier* † to follow as rapidly as she could. Surcouf reached the Isle of France in safety; but scarcely had he landed when he was informed that the Governor, M. de Malartic,

* The bill on presentation was not paid; the drawee contending that he had discovered that the transaction was illegal.

† The *Cartier* was re-captured in the Bay of Bengal by an English man-of-war.

had confiscated his prizes on the plea that he was unauthorised to make captures. Against such a ruling Surcouf appealed in person to the Directory. The case came before the Council of the Five Hundred, who, on the 4th September, 1797 (17 Fructidor, year V.) pronounced a decision in Surcouf's favour. His prizes, sold at the islands, had realised the sum of 1,700,000 francs; but certain difficulties having arisen regarding the question of exchange, Surcouf agreed to accept for himself and his crew the diminished sum of 660,000 francs. This amount was paid him.

Surcouf remained about fourteen months in France. Tired then of inaction, he obtained at Nantes the command of a privateer brig, called the *Clarisse,* mounting 14 guns and having a crew of 120 men. He set out with her in September for the Indian seas, and reached the line without sighting a vessel. Scarcely, however, had he entered the southern hemisphere when a sail was signalled. She proved to be an English three-masted vessel carrying 26 guns. The wind was in her favour, and she bore down with all sail on the *Clarisse.*

Here again destruction seemed inevitable. The prospect did not, however, appal Surcouf. He first exchanged broadsides with his enemy, then wearing, came down on the starboard tack and took up an advantageous position on his quarter. For half an hour the victory was obstinately contested, but at the end of that time, the stranger, having been considerably maltreated and having lost her captain, clapped on all sail and bore away. The *Clarisse* was in no condition to follow her.

The damages sustained on that occasion were quickly repaired, and Surcouf pursued his journey without interruption to the Indian seas. Still sailing eastward he captured, after a severe combat, two English merchant ships with rich cargoes. He returned with these to the island of Bourbon, the Isle of France being blockaded by British cruisers. Having there repaired and refitted the *Clarisse*, he sailed again (August, 1799) for the Straits. In this voyage he touched at Java, and landed there to replenish his water-tanks. Whilst on shore here with only a few of his crew, he was suddenly attacked by a chieftain of the country who came upon him with a large following. Unprepared and his crew unarmed, Surcouf owed his escape to the presence of mind which never failed him. Leaving his musket still slung across his shoulders he advanced towards the Javanese chieftain and placed in his hand a red handkerchief he had untied from his neck. The chieftain, whose actions up to that moment had denoted the greatest hostility, seemed so fascinated by the colour of the present he had received that he contented himself with making signs to Surcouf and his men to re-embark immediately. It need scarcely be added that the hint was promptly taken.

In the cruise which followed, the *Clarisse* captured a Danish ship carrying an English cargo, a Portuguese ship, and an English merchantman, the *Auspicious*.

A few days later Surcouf was in pursuit of another merchantman and was fast approaching her, when he perceived bearing down upon him from an opposite direction a vessel which was unmistakeably a ship of war.

This was no other than the English frigate *La Sybille* of 48 guns, which had but recently captured off the Sandheads the French frigate *La Forte* of 52 guns. Surcouf was apparently lost, as the English frigate soon showed herself a better sailer than the *Clarisse*. But he did not despair. He cast overboard his spare masts and spars; then eight of his heavy guns; and that not being sufficient he half-emptied his water casks. Thus lightened the *Clarisse* gained rapidly on the frigate and at daybreak the following morning the latter was completely out of sight. Two days later Surcouf captured an English merchantman, the *James*, laden with rice, and on the fourth day after that the American ship *Louisa*. With these captures Surcouf closed his career in the *Clarisse*. Returning with his prizes to the islands, he was offered the command of a new privateer, just arrived from Bordeaux, and reputed to be the fastest sailer afloat. Surcouf accepted the offer.

The new privateer was named *La Confiance*. She was of between 400 and 500 tons burden, and carried 16 guns. Her crew consisted of 159 Frenchmen, twenty-five volunteers from the island of Bourbon, and about twenty natives. She left the islands for her cruise in the Indian waters the middle of April 1800.

Surcouf went first to the Malabar coast on account of

the monsoon. But in July he directed thence his course towards Trincomali. Chased, though in vain, off that harbour by an English man-of-war, he pushed his way towards the mouths of the Ganges, having captured up to this time one American and two English merchantmen. He was off the Sandheads on 7th October when a sail was signalled to the eastward. Soon she was discerned to be a large and heavily armed ship. She was, in fact, the *Kent*, an Indiaman of 820 tons, carrying 26 guns, and having on board 437 Europeans, including troops.*

The *Kent* carelessly approached *La Confiance*, taking her to be a friend. Nor was it till she was within cannon-shot that her captain perceived his mistake. Still he made light of his enemy, and opening fire, in a very short space of time he inflicted severe damage on the hull, the rigging, and the masts of the Frenchman. Still Surcouf did not reply. It was his object to board, and he endeavoured to manœuvre in such a manner as to gain the port side of the *Kent*. When at length he had succeeded in this, he opened a tremendous broadside and musketry fire, then fastening the grappling-irons he attached himself closely to his enemy. Thenceforward,

* The French accounts state that besides twenty-six broadside guns, the *Kent* carried twelve on her quarter-deck and forecastle. James implies that this was not so. On the other hand, James reduces the number of the crew, including passengers, to about 140. But this is manifestly incorrect, for besides her own crew of more than 120, she had taken on board the entire crew of the *Queen*, an Indiaman burnt at St. Salvador, and she had besides, the troops and passengers of both vessels.

from her superior height out of the water, the fire of the *Kent* could only pass over the deck of *La Confiance*.

To climb on the enemy's deck followed by the crew, was a work of an instant. After a desperate conflict the English were driven below, their flag was hauled down, but still they did not give in. The fight continued below in the batteries, nor was it until resistance had become useless that it ceased, and the *Kent* surrendered.

In this battle the French had sixteen men wounded, of whom three died of their wounds. The English lost seventy men killed and wounded.* Surcouf at once transported the greater part of his prisoners, amongst whom was the daughter of the Margrave of Anspach married to an English general, on board a three-masted coasting vessel which opportunely came near enough to be captured; then placing sixty of his men under an officer on board the *Kent*, he sailed in company with her to the Islands. He arrived there in November. There, too, he received instructions to re-conduct the *Confiance* to France with a view to her receiving a more powerful armament. He sailed with this object on the 29th January 1801, and arrived at La Rochelle on the 13th April following, having captured a Portuguese vessel, the *Ebro*, carrying 18 twelve-pounders, on the way.

That same year the brief treaty of Amiens put a stop to hostilities. Surcouf then married. But the war being resumed in 1803, the First Consul offered him the commission of post captain (*capitaine de vaisseau*) in

* James says about fifty-eight.

the French Navy, with the command of two frigates in the Indian seas. In the interview which followed with the First Consul, Surcouf would only accord a provisional acceptance of the offer. "I am willing," he is reported to have said, "to undertake the duty, provided I am "made independent of all superior command, whether of "the admiral in the Indian seas, or of any senior officer "I may encounter." The First Consul declined to grant him a power so excessive; but struck by his manner and perfectly cognisant of his reputation he asked his opinion as to the policy by which the French Navy could be placed on such a footing as to cause the greatest injury to the English. The reply of Surcouf was eminently characteristic of the man: "If I were in your place," he replied, "I would burn all my line of battle ships; I "would never deliver battle to the English fleets and "squadrons. But I would construct and send into every "sea frigates and light ships in such extraordinary "numbers that the commerce of the enemy must be "speedily annihilated." Napoleon was then too much engaged with the project of the invasion of England, rendered abortive by the misconduct of Villeneuve, to depart so markedly from the established traditions of naval warfare; but he did not the less appreciate the intelligent ideas of the bold sailor. He conferred upon him the Cross of the Legion of Honour.

Until the year 1806 Surcouf remained in France, living on his savings, and sending out privateers commanded by his friends and relations. But in 1806 he became tired of inaction. He panted again for life on the Indian seas. He accordingly in that year had built under his own superintendence a vessel to carry 18 guns and a crew of 192 men. In this ship, which he called the *Revenant,* he sailed from St. Malo for the Indian waters on the 2nd March 1807.

The islands were reached, without any adventure worthy of note, on the 10th June. So great was the consternation in Calcutta on the news that this famous cruiser was on his way once again to the mouths of the Ganges, that the reward of a lakh of rupees was offered by the English Government for his capture.* But undeterred by this, Surcouf, on the 3rd September, sailed for his destination. On the 26th of the same month he arrived of Vizagapatam. The same day he captured the *Trafalgar*, a merchant ship laden with rice and carrying 12 guns, and the *Mangles* with a similar cargo and carrying 14 guns.† In the next

* I have been unable to discover the actual order; but the Indian journals for 1807 and 1808 abound with complaints of the injuries caused by Surcouf to the British trade. The *Asiatic Annual Register* records in October 1807 that the losses in the value of captured ships in the preceding six weeks, amounted to thirty lakhs of rupees.

† The *Asiatic Annual Register* (1808) states that these vessels were insured for 150,000 rupees each; that Surcouf sent their crews on shore detaining only the captains, and Mr. Nichol, who would appear to have been a person of some consideration. Subsequently Mr. Nichol managed to effect his escape in a manner, says the *Annual Register*, fair and honourable, yet such as was likely to cause great irritation to Surcouf. Yet the French captain would not allow his feelings to interfere with what he considered to be due to propriety. He took the first opportunity of forwarding to the British Government the whole of the personal property left by Mr. Nichol on board the ship.

few days the *Admiral Aplin*, the *Susanna*, the *Hunter*, the *Fortune* (previously captured from the French), and the *Success* struck their flags to him. Such was the terror he inspired that the Govenor-General in Council placed on all the vessels anchored in the Húghli an embargo to be binding as long as Surcouf might remain in the Bay of Bengal.

Hearing of this order Surcouf took an eastern course. On the 16th November he sighted three Indiamen conveying troops. These he avoided. But the next day he captured the *New Endeavour*,* laden with salt; and two days later the *Colonel Macauby*.† On the 12th December, returning from the Burmese waters, to which he had repaired without making a capture, he was chased, ineffectually, by a man-of-war and a corvette. Two days later he captured two brigs,‡ from whose masters he learned that the embargo had been taken off the English vessels in the Húghli. On the 17th he captured the *Sir William Burroughs* of 700 tons, laden with teak, and bound from Rangoon to Calcutta. He sent her to the islands. Early on the morning of the third subsequent day he found himself within cannon-shot of an English man-of-war. The smallest indication

* Surcouf ascertained that this vessel belonged to the captain who was navigating her, and that she was not insured. With a rare generosity he restored her to her owner unconditionally.

† From the *Colonel Macauby* Surcouf took 1440 bottles of claret, some specie and some gunpowder. He then restored her to her owner for the same reason which had prompted his restoration of the *New Endeavour*.

‡ These brigs were restored to their owners.

of fear would have lost him. But Surcouf was quite equal to the occasion. He steadily pursued his course, unquestioned and unmolested, his true character unsuspected, and he soon sailed out of sight. A few days later he captured a Portuguese vessel, the *Oriente*, and a fine ship under Arab colours, but whose papers attested her to be English property. Both these vessels were likewise despatched to the islands.* His crew being reduced to seventy men, and he having received intelligence that a new English frigate had arrived with the express mission to capture him, Surcouf resolved to follow his prizes thither. Chased, though ineffectually, by an English man-of-war, he arrived at Port St. Louis on the 31st January 1808, and found that all his prizes had safely preceded him.

Surcouf shortly afterward set out for France in a vessel called the *Charles*† with a cargo valued at five millions of francs. His vessel, the *Revenant*,‡ after a short cruise under her first lieutenant, Potier, had been

* Thither also had been despatched all the captures not specially referred to in the text, except the *Admiral Aplin*, shipwrecked on the Coromandel coast, the *Hunter*, which he abandoned, and the *Success*, which he burned.

† The *Charles* was an old frigate called *La Semillante*, worn out in service, and sold for the purposes of commerce.

‡ The fate of the *Revenant* was curious. After a short cruise under the command of Potier, in which she captured a Portuguese frigate, the *Conceção de San Antonio*, pierced for 64, and carrying 54 guns, she was taken up by the Governor, added to the French Navy as a corvette of 22 guns, and re-named the *Jena*. In this new form she sailed with an envoy and despatches for the Persian Gulf, captured the schooner *Swallow* with 2500 dollars on board her, and the *Janet*, a small country

taken up by the Governor, General Decaën, for the defence of the islands, and there appeared to be no chance of a further cruise in the Indian waters.* He reached St. Malo on the 5th February 1809. In a few days he went to Paris where he recived a flattering reception from the Minister of Marine.

His active life on the sea was now terminated. The capture shortly afterwards by the British of the Isles of France and Bourbon tended very much to shut out the French cruisers from the Indian seas. Surcouf continued, nevertheless, during the war to arm and fit out privateers.† When peace came he devoted himself to maritime commerce, to agriculture, and to shooting.

Surcouf died in 1827. "France," writes M. Cunat, in his admirable biography, "lost in him a distinguished " warrior; the naval service one of her bravest captains; " and St. Malo, his native town, an illustrious offspring. " Whilst the tears of the unfortunate proclaimed his " charity, his fellow citizens felt deeply the loss they

craft, but had herself to succumb to the *Modeste*, a frigate of greatly superior force, which she had approached in the belief that she was a merchant ship. The *Jena* was added to the English Navy, under the name of the *Victor*.—*Asiatic Annual Regisier*.

James states that the *Modeste* carried 36 guns; and the *Jena* 18. Seven of these, together with her boats, hencoops, and spars, she threw overboard in her attempt to escape.

* As I am not writing a life of Surcouf, I do not propose to enter upon the snbject of his disputes with the Governor, especially as the Emperor Napoleon gave a decision in his favour.

† Amongst the most successful of his privateering ventures were the *Auguste*, the *Dorade*, the *Biscayenne*, the *Edoard*, the *Espadon*, the *Ville de Caën*, the *Adolphe*, and the *Renard*.

" had sustained. Their regrets were a last homage to " the man whose enterprise, as a sailor, had astonished " the world, and who, as a trader, had benefited all the " industries of the country which he idolised." It would be difficult to add a word to this eloquent eulogy.

II.

A CONTEMPORARY, a fellow-townsman, and almost to the same extent a destroyer of English commerce on the Indian waters, was François Thomas Lemême, whose adventures I am now about to record.

Born in 1763 at St. Malo, Lemême enrolled himself as a volunteer on board the privateer the *Prince de Mombany*, commanded by one Boynard. This was during the war for the independence of the United States, when opportunities offered to the sons of Brittany and of Normandy to prey upon the commerce of the great rival of France. The cruise of the *Prince de Mombany* was not altogether fortunate. She took, indeed, some merchantmen, but she was forced herself to succumb to an English frigate; "and it was in the "prisons of Great Britain," says M. Gallois, "that "Lemême learned, in his early youth, to hate with a "hatred altogether national the islanders whom he was "destined later often to encounter and to overcome."

Released from his British prison by the treaty of Versailles, Lemême continued his seafaring life. He happened to be at the Isle of France in 1793 in command of a small transport brig, the *Hirondelle*, when the intelligence arrived that war had been declared between France and England. Instantly Lemême transformed the *Hirondelle* into a privateer. He armed her with twelve 4-pounder carronades, and manned her with eighty men. In addition to these, volunteers pressed forward to serve under him; of them, however, he could take only thirty.

Thus armed and manned, Lemême sailed from the islands in July, 1793, taking the direction of the Indian Ocean. On the 16th August he encountered and carried by boarding a Dutch corvette carrying eighteen 9-pounders, called *The Good Werwagting*. It is related that before Lemême had been able to lay the *Hirondelle* alongside her powerful opponent the fire from the latter had so damaged the French privateer, that one of her officers remarked to the captain that the enemy's fire would sink her. "That's just what I want," remarked Lemême, "we shall be obliged then to put our feet on "the decks of that one." Immediately afterwards he brought the *Hirondelle* alongside and boarded.

Nine days later, in company with and aided by his prize, Lemême attacked, and, after a contest of forty minutes, captured the *William Thesied*, a large Dutch Indiaman, pierced for 60 but carrying only 40 guns. With these two prizes Lemêne returned to the islands.

He did not stay there long. Transferred from the *Hirondelle* to the *Ville de Bordeaux*, carrying 32 guns, and having on board a crew of 200 men, Lemême started again in the month of October for his old cruising ground. Proceeding direct to Sumatra, he stormed the fortifications of Padang, one of the Mantawi islands close to the mainland, and seized all the shipping lying off it. Obtaining most advantageous terms from the Dutch Governor, he quitted Padang, his ship well laden with the products of the expedition, and returned to the Isle of France, capturing on his way a Portuguese merchantman, the *Santo Sacramento*. The share of the plunder accruing to Lemêne from this expedition amounted to 1,100,000 francs, equal to £44,000 sterling.

In the *Amphitrite*, of which he next took command, Lemême made several rich captures; but of the particulars I have been unable to obtain a record. Transferred again to *L'Uni*, carrying 21 guns and a crew of 200 men, he became the terror of the Indian seas. She is reported to have captured in her short cruise six merchantmen, two of which carried very valuable cargoes, and four native *grabs** all laden with specie. Lemême, however, having placed insufficient prize crews on board these, the Moplahs, who had originally manned them, rose upon and killed their captors. Amongst the letters found on the body of the chief officer was one from Lemême to the owners of *L'Uni*, in which he announced his intention "to sweep "the Malabar and Coromandel coasts and to call at

* A *grab* is a three-masted vessel peculiar in those days to the Malabar coast.

"Tranquebar for refreshments."* He would appear to have kept his word.

After the return of *L'Uni* to the islands, Lemême made two more cruises in the Indian seas, the first in the *Clarisse;* the second in the *Grande Hirondelle.* The cruise in the *Clarisse* was at least as successful as the cruises which had preceded hers. Hostile ships of war were successfully avoided and merchantmen were successfully encountered. But the same fortune did not attend the *Grande Hirondelle.* After making three captures, she herself was forced to succumb, on the 31st December, 1801, to the British frigate *La Sybille,* 48 guns, commanded by Captain Charles Adam.†

Released from confinement by the treaty of Amiens, Lemême, who had realised an enormous fortune by his cruises, renounced the sea, and started as a merchant. But he managed his affairs so unsuccessfully, that when the war broke out again in 1803, he had lost all he had possessed. Again he resumed his earlier profession, and hoisting his flag on board a three-masted vessel, the *Fortune,* carrying 12 guns and a crew of 160 men, he

* *Asiatic Annual Register.*

† The fact of the capture of the *Grande Hirondelle* when under the command of Lemême has been ignored by all the French authorities I have been able to consult. In his biographical sketch of Lemême M. Gallois merely mentions that before the peace of Amiens he had cruised in the *Clarisse* and *Grande Hirondelle.* Yet I have before me not only Captain Adam's official report of the capture, dated 2nd January, 1802, but also a letter from Lemême himself, dated the 7th *idem,* written when a prisoner, and addressed to Captain Adam himself. —*Asiatic Annual Register,* 1802, pages 42, 45, 46.

made his way, towards the end of 1803, to the Bay of Bengal.

This time his success was unexampled. In a very brief period he captured at least fifteen vessels.* The sums realised by the sale of these was enormous, the official returns showing that the first six on the list sold for nearly 1,200,000 francs. Yet, unfortunately for Lemême, he did not live to enjoy his gains. On the 7th November 1804, in the waters of the Arabian sea, he found himself early in the morning in close proximity to the *Concorde*, a British frigate carrying 48 guns, which had been sent from Bombay in search of him. In vain he attempted to escape. The *Concorde* was a better sailer, and at half-past three o'clock she came within range. Lemême did all that man could do to cripple his adversary. But it was useless. At half-past ten o'clock, his ship reduced to a wreck, he had to strike his flag.

With this action ended his career. Shipped, the 15th February 1805, on board the *Walthamstow* as a prisoner

* The official report of Admiral Linois, published in the *Moniteur*, gives a list of ten, viz., the *Barlow*, the *Eleonora*, the *Active*, the *Pomona*, the *Vulcan*, the *Mahomed Bux*, the *Nancy*, the *Creole*, the *Fly*, and the *Shrewsbury*. M. Gallois adds to this list the *Industry*, a packet boat, restored to its owner; the *Bembow*, the *Daos*, and the *Lionne*. In the *Asiatic Annual Register* for March, 1804, I find the following: "On the 1st ultimo the *Taxbux*, under Arab colours, was fired at, and at nine p.m. taken possession of by the French privateer *La Fortune*, commanded by Citizen Lemême. * * * Captain Mercer was informed on board the privateer that she had taken three vessels, the *Sarah*, the *Eliza*, and the *Active*." The *Taxbux* was restored to Captain Mercer.

bound for England, he died on the way (30th March). In him Franch lost one of the most daring of her sailor adventurers, and the Anglo-Indian community were relieved of the obligation to give to the question, as to the name of the privateersman by whom their last merchant vessel had been captured, the stereotyped reply of "*toujours lemême*."

But little inferior to Lemême as a destroyer of British commerce in the Indian seas was Jean Dutertre. In the chronicle of the *Asiatic Annual Register* for November 1799, there appeared the following notice:—"On Monday " morning, the 28th October last, an express arrived at " the General Post Office, Bombay, from Masulipatam, " conveying accounts of the capture of the under- " mentioned ships by a French privateer, a little, to the " northward of the Madras Roads, *viz.*, the Nawab of " Arcot's ship, *Surprise* galley, the *Princess Royal*, " formerly a Company's ship, the *Thomas*, ditto, an " extra ship, the *Joyce*, belonging to Masulipatam, " the *Lord Hobart*, belonging to Madras. * * * " The privateer by which these ships were captured is " supposed to be the *Malartic*, mounting 12 guns, " and commanded by the same person who took the " Danish ship *Haabat* on the coast four months ago."

The supposition was correct. The privateer was the *Malartic*, carrying 12 guns, having a crew of 110 men, and commanded by Jean Dutertre. Dutertre was born at Lorient and early took to the sea. He happened to be at the Isle of France when the *Emilie* arrived there in charge of the prizes which Surcouf had taken in her. Surcouf, it may be recollected, had abandoned her for his prize, the *Cartier*. Dutertre was then appointed to her command, and in her he made one or two cruises, the details regarding which are altogether wanting. He was next heard of as commanding the *Malartic*, in which he made the prizes to which I have alluded, and subsequently, in addition, he captured the *Governor North* and the *Marquess Wellesley*. Shortly afterwards, however, the *Malartic* was forced to strike her colours to an English vessel of superior force, the *Phœnix*, and Dutertre was taken prisoner to England.

Released by the peace of Amiens Dutertre recommen his career in the Indian seas. He again became the terror of those waters. In concert with another adventurer named Courson, he, in one season, captured the *Rebecca*, the *Active*, the *Clarendon*, the *William*, the *Betsey Jane*, the *Henry Addington*, the *Admiral Rainier*, the *Lady William Bentinck*, the *Nancy*, the *Actæon*, the *Brothers*, the *Hebe*, the *Mongamah*, and the *Warren Hastings*. So great was the consternation caused that we find the English journals of the period complaining that "there is no part of the world, not-
" withstanding the superiority of the English marine,
" in which the enemy does not succeed in molesting
" our navigation, and in causing us infinite losses."

It was, after all, but the natural consequence of the system of privateering thus affecting the power which carried the commerce of the world.

After this cruise, which began in 1804 and closed the following year, Dutertre entered the French Navy and became lost to the public view. He died in 1811.

Amongst the other adventurers who caused great damage to English commerce, I find the Courson, above referred to, and who, previous to the peace of Amiens, had made several captures and had been taken prisoner and sent to England; Potier of St. Malo, who succeeded Surcouf in the *Revenant*, and who, in command of that privateer carrying 18 guns, captured the Portuguese man-of-war, the *Conceção*, pierced for 64, but carrying 54 guns; and Mallerouse of St. Malo, who commanding the *Iphigénie* of 18 guns, and having captured the *Pearl*, Indiaman, carrying 10 guns and having on board treasure amounting to more than three lakhs of rupees, found himself suddenly face to face with H. M.'s ship *Trincomali*, carrying 18 24-pounder carronades. The combat which ensued was so remarkable that I make no apology for recording it at length. I am fortunately able to quote an authority which every Englishman will recognise as impartial, for the extract which follows is taken from a private letter written to his brother in England by Mr. Cramlington, who was chief officer of the *Pearl* when she was captured, and at the time a prisoner on board the *Iphigénie*.

After recounting the story of the capture of the *Pearl* Mr. Cramlington thus continues: "The treasure was " shifted on board the privateer the next day; and they " were so elated with their success that they determined "to return from their cruise immediately. But on the "10th, at night, we fell in with H. M.'s ship *Trincomali*, "Captain Rowe, mounting 18 24-pounder carronades, "but badly manned.* She had been fitted out at "Bombay, and had been cruising in the Gulf nine or "ten months; her crew very sickly, had lost a number "of them by death, and had no fresh supply. I have "been told she had only seventy active men on board.

"A partial action took place the next day as they "passed each other, and on the 12th, at three P.M., "they came within gunshot again, and kept firing at "each other till after sunset, but at too great a distance "for much damage to be done. Owing to calm and "light airs they could not get near each other. A "schooner, named the *Comet*, was in company with the "*Trincomali*, mounting 8 small guns. The captain of "the privateer wanted very much to cut her off, but "through the bravery and good conduct of her captain "all his schemes failed, and she served to engage the "*Pearl* for whom she was more than a match.

"At half-past six o'clock the same evening, a fine "breeze springing up, the privateer bore down towards "her prize. The *Trincomali* followed, and at ten P.M. "(being moonlight) brought her to action, which con-

* James, in his *Naval History*, writes quite at random regarding the armament of the combatants. He speaks of the *Trincomali* as carrying 16 guns, *probably* 6-pounders (the italics are mine); and of the *Iphigénie* as carrying 22 guns. The French captain he calls "Malroux." Compare his account with that given by the English eye witness in the text.

" tinued for two hours with great fury within musket-
" shot; when with one ship luffing up, and the other
" edging down, they fell alongside each other and
" grappled muzzle and muzzle. In this situation they
" remained about half an hour, the slaughter very great
" on both sides. The French, being more numerous,
" were preparing to board, when by some fatal accident,
" the *Trincomali* blew up, and every soul on board
" perished, except one English seaman, named Thomas
" Dawson, and a lascar. The explosion was so great,
" and the ships so close, that the privateer's broadside
" was stove in.

" I leave you to judge the dreadful situation I was in
" at this crisis; being below two decks, in the square
" of the main-hatchway, in the place appointed for the
" wounded, which was full of poor souls of that
" description in circumstances too shocking to be
" described. All at once the hatchway was filled in with
" wood, the lights were driven out, the water rushing in,
" and no visible passage to the deck. The ship appeared
" to be shaken to pieces, as the hold beams had shrunk so
" considerably, that where there was room before to
" stand nearly upright, you could now only crawl on hands
" and knees, which I did towards the hole on the side
" where the water was coming in. Close to this, by the
" light of the moon, I found a hole through both decks,
" which had been newly made, I suppose, by the falling
" of some of the *Trincomali's* guns, or other wreck.
" Through this I got with difficulty upon deck, when I

" found the ship just disappearing forward, and hastened " aft as fast as I could over the bodies of the killed, with " which the deck was covered, to the tafferel, and jumped " overboard.

" I swam a little way from her, dreading the suction, " and looked round for her, but she had totally dis- " appeared. I afterwards caught hold of a piece of " wood to which I clung for about an hour and a half, " and at which time the boats of the *Pearl* came to " pick us up, there being about thirty Frenchmen in the " same predicament. They, however, were all taken up " first; and when I solicited to be taken in, I had a " blow made at my head with an oar, which luckily " missed me. This treatment I met with from two " different boats, and I began to think they were going " to leave me to my fate. But the French officer in " command of the *Pearl*, hearing there were some " Englishmen on the wreck, ordered the boats im- " mediately to return and take us up, *viz.*, myself and " Thomas Dawson, then the only survivor of the " *Trincomali*.

" There were killed and drowned on board the " *Iphigénie* 115 or 120 men. Among whom were the " captain, seven officers, the surgeon, two young men, " volunteers from the Isle of France, the first boatswain, " gunner, and carpenter. All the treasure went down " in the privateer. Captain Rowe of the *Trincomali* " was killed before his ship blew up, as was also the " first lieutenant whose name was Williams. The

" *Comet*, immediately on the accident happening, made " sail from the *Pearl*.* I suppose she was afraid there " might be too many French for her to manage. On " the 15th we arrived here " (Muscat) " for water, &c., " and the French officer was so good as to give me my " liberty."

The *Pearl* subsequently reached the Isle of France in safety, but the career of Mallerouse was over.

In addition to the preceding I may mention Pinaud of Nantes. One incident in the career of this brave adventurer deserves to be recorded.

In my notice of Surcouf I have mentioned the feats he was able to accomplish in the *Clarisse*, a brig carrying 14 guns. When Surcouf left the *Clarisse* for the *Confiance*, the command of the former was entrusted to Pinaud. Pinaud took her in 1800 to the Indian seas, made many captures, but was forced himself to succumb to an English man-of-war. Taken to Madras, he was thrown into prison, and finally placed, with about 600 other prisoners, on board the *Prince*, Indiaman, to be taken to England under the convoy of a squadron of six ships of war returning thither. The convoy sailed the

* James says that the *Pearl* escaped from the *Comet*. It would appear from the impartial statement of the Englishman in the text, the *Comet* fled from the *Pearl*. But let the facts speak. The *Pearl* remaining on the scene of action picked up by successive trips of her boats about thirty Frenchmen and two Englishmen. The captain of the *Comet*, in his official report, dated 18th February 1800, admits that he only picked four sepoys and a lascar, and those immediately after the accident! It is clear from this that it was not the *Pearl* which sailed first from the scene of the encounter.

middle of 1801, and reached in safety the latitude of the Isle of France. The locality Pinaud considered favourable, if other circumstances should combine, to strike a blow for freedom. He communicated his plan to his companions. They approved. It so happened that on the 29th October the squadron was surprised, when near the Isle of France, by a heavy squall which dispersed the vessels composing it. Pinaud considered the moment opportune. The chief officer was in the fore-topmast crosstrees; the second officer in charge of the deck; the captain, the military officers, and two French officers (prisoners) were in the cuddy taking tea, when suddenly there rushed upon them Pinaud at the head of a strong party of prisoners. Another division at the same time took possession of the deck. The surprise had been so well managed and the secret so well kept that there was not even the semblance of a struggle. Pinaud took command of the ship, followed the course laid down for some time so as not to excite suspicion, then, when night fell, he put out all the lights, changed the ship's course, and reached the Isle of France a few weeks later (20th November). Pinaud next made a most successful cruise in the *Subtile*. He subsequently transferred his cruising ground to the West Indies.

It would be a tale of repetition to recount the deeds of several other adventurers, such as Cautance of the *Eugéne;* Peron of the *Bellone;* and Henri of the *Henriette*. It will suffice to state that the injury inflicted on the British trade with the East was enormous, and the gain to the French so immediate that the privateers continued to increase and prosper in spite of our overwhelming naval superiority.

III.

The secret of their impunity lay in the fact that in the Isles of France and Bourbon the enemy's cruisers possessed a strong base of operations. It was the charmed refuge to which they could retire; from which they could issue with renewed strength. It may be asked why the British, boasting as they did of the command of the seas, allowed those islands to remain so long in the possession of their deadliest enemy. The question is difficult, even at this distant period, to answer. The sagacious intellect of Marquess Wellesley had early detected the weak point in the British armour, and with characteristic vigour he had at once applied himself to repair it. Very soon after the fall of Seringapatam he had organised from the armies of the three presidencies a force which, massed at Trincomali, should proceed thence to the conquest of Java and of the French islands. This expedition had been on the very point of setting out when urgent orders from England, despatched overland, diverted it to Egypt to aid the expeditionary corps of Sir Ralph Abercromby. Partly, probably, owing to the "timid "counsels" which supervened on the departure of the great Marquess from India; partly, likewise, on account of the exaggerated opinion entertained in England of the strength of the islands and of the great difficulties which would attend an expedition, the idea was allowed for some years to drop. The British Government contented itself with spasmodic directions to blockade the islands—a measure, the effective carrying out of which was impossible, and which, even when attempted, did not affect the successful egress and ingress of the adventurous cruisers.

At length the damage done by those cruisers aroused a cry of indignation and despair to which it was impossible that the Government should remain longer deaf. Under the pressure thus excited the Governor-General, Lord Minto, urged upon the Home Government the necessity of adopting measures more effectual than that of a blockade by ships depending for their supplies on the Cape or on Bombay. Lord Minto was in consequence authorised to occupy Rodriguez, a small island about 300 miles to the eastward of the Isle of France. Still neither the English Government nor the Governor-General entertained any idea beyond gaining a base from which to supply blockading squadrons. In accordance with these views a small force, consisting of 200 Europeans and 200 natives, under the command of Lieutenant-Colonel Keating, was despatched in May, 1809, from Bombay, in H.M.'s ship *Belliqueux*, to occupy Rodriguez.

Rodriguez, used by the French as a garden to supply

the larger islands with vegetables, was garrisoned by three Frenchmen, gardeners, and these were insufficient, even if they had been inclined, to offer any serious resistance. The English detachment, therefore, occupied the island, without opposition, the 4th August. They kept the French gardeners to grow vegetables on its soil, whilst using the island also as a depôt for ships' stores. These were landed in great numbers.

It was soon found, however, that the French privateers still sailed and returned with their prizes as they had been accustomed to sail and to return. They continued to elude, as successfully as they had before eluded, the vigilance of the British cruisers. In a word, it was found that even with a base so near to the scene of operations as was Rodriguez effectual blockade of the islands was impossible.

Under these circumstances the garrison of Rodriguez was strengthened, and Colonel Keating was authorised to make an attempt on the Isle of Bourbon.* That officer accordingly embarked on the 16th September (1809) 368 officers and men, of whom one-half belonged to the 2nd Bombay Native Infantry, on board H.M.'s ships *Néréide* and *Otter* and the Honourable Company's cruiser *Wasp*. On the 18th these three vessels arrived off Port Louis, and the following morning they joined

* This island was then called "Bonaparte," and was subsequently named and has since been known as "Reunion;" but for the sake of uniformity I adhere to the nomenclature it bore from the time of its first occupation by the French.

H.M.'s ships *Raisonnable* and *Sirius;* the naval force being commanded by Commodore Rowley of the former. That same day the seamen and troops destined for the attack, amounting to 604 men, were massed on board the *Néréide*, and towards evening the squadron stood for the Isle of Bourbon, off the eastern coast of which it arrived on the morning of the 20th. Colonel Keating, however, had resolved to attempt to carry St. Paul, the chief town on the western side, to secure the batteries there, and to force the surrender of the enemy's shipping in the port.

At five o'clock on the morning of the 21st the troops were disembarked to the south of Point de Galotte, seven miles from St. Paul. They were formed into three columns: the reserve, composed of eighty men of the Pompadours and eighty of the Royal Marines, under the command of Captain Forbes; the second column, consisting of the detail of the 2nd Battalion 2nd Bombay Native Infantry, under the command of Captain Imlack; the centre column formed of 100 sailors under Captain Willoughby, and of the remainder of the Pompadours and Marines, about 140 in number, under Captain Hanna.

Colonel Keating landed first with the reserve to cover the disembarkation of the other two columns. This having been effected, the reserve column was directed to proceed under Captain Forbes by the road leading to St. Paul, until it should pass the bridge over the lake, when it was to make a turn to the left, and take possession first of the barracks, then of the second battery, La Pierre, and then to proceed on to the first battery, La Centière, where it would receive fresh orders from the commanding officer; the second column, under Captain Imlack, was directed to pass the river Galotte and to proceed along the seashore until it should reach the rivulet running from the lake into the bay. It was to advance thence up the bed of the rivulet, past the right flank of the battery, Lambouçère, then move out and form towards the sea, thus bringing it within pistol-shot of the rear of the battery, of which Captain Imlack was to take possession, spike the guns, and move on to La Centière.

The centre column under Colonel Keating was to march straight on the battery La Centière, and to occupy it, detaching thence a force to take possession of the battery La Neuve. La Centière was to constitute the post on which all attacks were to concentrate.

Whilst the British troops are marching in the order above indicated, I propose to take a glance at the means possessed by the French commandant of the island to resist so formidable an invasion.

The commander of the French force in the island of Bourbon was General des Bruslys. That force was very small. There were concentrated at the capital, St. Denis, under the personal command of General des Bruslys, about 100 troops of the line and 300 Creoles. At St. Paul there were on board the frigate *Caroline*, anchored in the harbour, 110 troops of the line and from 200 to 300

Creoles. The remainder of the force, entirely Creole, was scattered over nine districts,* from which they could not without difficulty be suddenly withdrawn and concentrated on a given point. Des Bruslys was expecting an attack not at St. Paul but at St. Denis. His lieutenant at the former place, the Commandant St. Michiel, had received no intimation that the English were about to land. When they did land he had not then even withdrawn from the *Caroline* the European troops on board of her.

It can easily be conceived then that Colonel Keating's first attack was successful. The second column took possession of the battery Lamboucère, and the centre column of the battery La Centière without any strong opposition, except that offered by the fire from the enemy's ships in the river. The reserve column had likewise moved on La Centière and had turned its guns on the enemy's shipping. The second column, under Captain Imlack, consisting only of 142 men of the 2nd Bombay Native Infantry and of twelve Europeans, was then sent to take possession of the battery La Neuve, deserted by the enemy.

But before Captain Imlack could reach La Neuve the French appeared on the field. Very early that morning the Commandant St. Michiel had ordered the disembarkation of the 110 Europeans from the *Caroline*, and had directed them to join him as soon as possible

* These were St. Leu, St. Louis, St. Pierre, St. Joseph, St. Rose, St. Benoit, St. André, St. Suzanne, and St. Marie.

in a very strong position he had taken up in front of the battery La Neuve. This position was covered by a stone wall carefully loop-holed, and flanked on both sides by a strong natural defence. Each of these flanks was again covered by three 6-pounders.

This position had been occupied by St. Michiel whilst the English were marching on the batteries Lamboucère and La Centière. He occupied it still with about 150 Creoles when the swarthy sons of India under their English officers marched upon it. The attack was conducted with great gallantry, but the defences were too strong and the artillery fire too concentrated, and the sepoys fell back. A second attack was not more successful. The British centre column, consisting entirely of Europeans, was then ordered up to reinforce the native troops. Again the attacking party charged. This time they succeeded, after a desperate conflict, in taking two of the enemy's guns, but they made no impression on his position. It was now the turn of the French to be reinforced. They were joined by 110 Europeans from the *Caroline*, and by many Creoles from the hills. The contest was now resumed with greater fury than ever, and it became necessary for the English commander to bring up the reserve under Captain Forbes. This officer, advancing by a circuitous route, occupied the battery La Neuve and thus took up a position very nearly in rear of the enemy.

St. Michiel felt his post no longer tenable. He evacuated it therefore, and fell back upon St. Paul;

losing, after a most gallant resistance, his four remaining guns. After that the course of the English was easy. The fourth and fifth batteries, La Pierre and La Caserne, fell into their hands. By half-past eight they had taken possession of the town evacuated by St. Michiel, the magazines, eight brass field pieces, 117 new and heavy iron guns of different calibres, and all the stores. The commodore, seeing the success of the troops, immediately stood in, anchored close to the enemy's shipping, and compelled it to surrender. The same evening Colonel Keating destroyed all the public property in the town not fit for transport, and re-embarked his troops.

General des Bruslys learned with surprise the same night the landing of the British troops on the west coast of the island. He immediately collected all his available men and marched towards St. Paul. He arrived on the hills covering the town on the evening of the 22nd and encamped there. Colonel Keating determined to dislodge him the following morning. He accordingly embarked his entire force in boats early on the 23rd. But whether it was that des Bruslys thought that further resistance would only lead to greater disaster, or whether the moral tension was too strong for him, this at least is certain, that he did not wait for a contest, but retreated to St. Denis and shot himself.*

* He left a paper saying that he had destroyed himself to avoid death on the scaffold,—a commentary on the dread caused in a weak mind by the terrible knowledge that his master required, before all things, success.

The Commandant St. Michiel succeeded to the post thus vacated by des Bruslys. There was nothing left for him but to negotiate with the conqueror. The conditions insisted upon by the latter were not heavy. It was arranged that he should retain possession of St. Paul until he should be able to place on board his ships the stores he had taken there, and to fit out the captured vessels* for sea. This was soon accomplished, and on the 2nd October Colonel Keating evacuated the island and set sail for Rodriguez.

* These were the *Caroline* frigate, 44 guns; the *Grappler* brig, 11 guns; the *Streatham* a merchantman, 850 tons and pierced for 30 guns; *l'Europe*, 820 tons, pierced for 26 guns; the *Fanny*, 150 tons; the *Très Amis* and *La Créole* of 60 tons each.

IV.

THE success of this expedition showed the Government how far from formidable were the resources possessed by the islands, and how easy it would be to strike a decisive blow at these harbours of safety for the French privateers. Impressed with this idea Lord Minto, without waiting for orders from England, dispatched in the spring of 1810, considerable reinforcements from the three presidences to the island of Rodriguez. These reinforcements raised the troops under Colonel Keating's orders to 3650 men, of whom not quite one-half were Europeans. So confident was Lord Minto of the success of his plans that he nominated, in anticipation, Mr. Farquhar of the Bengal Civil Service to be Governor of the island.

The transports conveying the reinforcements to Colonel Keating arrived off Rodriguez on the 25th June, but it was not till the 3rd July that the expedition was able to start for its destination. This time Colonel Keating had determined to strike at once at the heart of Bourbon, at its capital, St. Denis. With this view it was arranged that the transports should meet at a given point about fifty miles to the windward of the island; that the troops should then concentrate by brigades on board H. M.'s ships of war* and that these should proceed at once to the points marked out for each beforehand.

About four o'clock on the afternoon of the 7th July, Lieutenant-Colonel Campbell and 150 troops of the 4th brigade, accompanied by Captain Willoughby, R.N., commanding a party of sailors, the whole constituting the advanced guard of the force, were successfully landed at a point between the battery St. Marie and the batteries of the town. A few moments later, Lieutenant-Colonel Macleod, commanding the 3rd brigade, effected a landing with 150 men, somewhat to the right of Colonel Campbell's party, expecting to be joined by the remainder of his brigade. But just at this moment the weather, which till then had been calm and moderate, suddenly became stormy. So violent was the surf that further disembarkation was impossible. Under these circumstances Colonel Keating could not fail to be very anxious for the safety of the handful of troops which had but just landed. Impressed, however, with the truth of the motto that in all doubtful circumstances boldness is prudence, the colonel was desirous that his troops should try to daunt the enemy by themselves taking the initiative. But the violence of the surf had increased and was increasing. No boat could take an order to them. Yet the fate of the 300 or 400 men just landed seemed to depend upon their receiving one. Every

* These were the *Boadicea*, 38; the *Sirius;* the *Iphigenia;* the *Magicienne;* and the *Néréide*.

device was tried. A small vessel was beached, stern foremost, in the hope that one at least of her crew might make his way to the shore. But the fury of the elements frustrated even this attempt. Further effort appeared impossible. Colonel Keating was in despair. At this crisis Lieutenant Foulstone of H.M.'s 69th Regiment came forward unsolicited, and volunteered to swim through the surf and carry orders to Colonel Macleod. His offer was promptly accepted. Carried in a boat to the edge of the surf Foulstone jumped in, and, though a good deal knocked about, reached the shore. He conveyed to Colonel Macleod the order to unite the two parties which had landed and at once to attack and storm St. Marie. Macleod carried out these instructions with spirit and energy, occupied the post, and remained there unmolested all night.

As the weather next day showed no signs of moderating, Colonel Keating proceeded with the 3rd and 4th brigades to the leeward, to Grand Chaloupe; where, on the 8th, about eleven a.m., he succeeded in effecting a landing. Colonel Keating at this point was separated from the town by heights. He lost no time in crossing these, and before two p.m. he occupied a position from which he could command the enemy's intrenchments.

But affairs had gone somewhat too fast for him. The 1st brigade, commanded by Colonel Fraser, had succeeded at two o'clock on the afternoon of the 7th in effecting a landing in a position to the south of the capital within sight of the enemy. This daring achievement had the effect of concentrating upon Colonel Fraser the entire attention of the French commandant, and diverting it from Colonel Macleod's isolated party. Colonel Fraser resolved to keep his attention fixed. He at once pushed forward, dislodged the enemy from the heights, and then took up a commanding position just above the town.

He had with him only 350 bayonets, all Europeans, but with these he kept the enemy anxious and occupied until darkness fell. He then retreated to a secure position a little in the rear which cut the communications between St. Denis and St. Paul.

Reinforced during the night by from 300 to 400 sepoys, and by his guns and pioneers, Colonel Fraser, posting the sepoys so as to protect his rear, advanced at four o'clock in the morning towards the town, re-occupied the position of the previous evening, and forming his troops there, waited for the day.

When day broke Fraser saw in the plain below him the whole available French force. This force, consisting of 190 Europeans and 350 Creoles, was drawn up in two columns, each with a field piece at its head, covered by the concentrated fire of the batteries, and commanded by the successor of the unfortunate des Bruslys, Colonel de Suzanne. Fraser did not hesitate. Under a mixed shower of balls issuing all at once from the many and deep-toned mouths of the ordnance and musketry* the

* *Asiatic Annual Register.*

British soldiers descended the heights in steady and unbroken alignment. When they reached the plain Colonel Fraser gave the order to charge. They at once charged home.

The French stood firm, covered by their guns, till the rush of the British grenadiers warned them of the earnestness of the play. They then retired in good order, without waiting for actual contact, behind the guns. But even there they were not safe from their infuriated enemy. Where they could retire he could follow. And he did follow. The dash of the onset could not be withstood. The French commandant escaped with difficulty; the second in command was taken prisoner; the men were driven headlong from position to position until all their redoubts were occupied by their victorious rivals, and though rallying, they did make an effort to recover these, the attempt was not only unsuccessful, but it cost them the life of their leader. Shortly afterwards the French commandant sent a cartel asking for terms. A little later Colonel Fraser was joined by the second brigade under Colonel Drummond.

Such was the position when Colonel Keating, with the 3rd and 4th brigades, came within sight of St. Denis on the afternoon of the 8th September. He was about to march on the town when a messenger from Colonel Fraser brought him the intelligence of its surrender.

The formal capitulation was not indeed signed till the evening of the following day. By the terms of it the entire island of Bourbon, containing a population of upwards of 100,000 souls, became British territory. This conquest had been effected with a loss of only eighteen men killed and seventy-nine wounded. There was no further resistance. The French troops were transported as prisoners of war to the Cape.

V.

The news of the capture of Bourbon reached Calcutta on the 24th August. It had the effect of stimulating the determination to conquer the larger island. It was known that the French squadron charged with the protection of the two islands, and consisting of the *Bellone* and *Minerve* frigates, and the sloop *Victor*, was absent on a cruise in the Indian seas. Mr. Farquhar, the new Governor of Bourbon, considered then the moment opportune, even before he should receive official authority, to feel his way towards the accomplishment of this greater work. Accordingly on the 13th August he embarked 250 men on board the boats of the frigates at his disposal, and sent them that night to attempt the surprise of the Isle de la Passe. This small island, distant only three miles from the mainland, lies at the entrance of the harbour of Grand Port, then called Port Imperial, on the south-eastern coast of the Isle of France. The expedition was successful, and a garrison of 130 men was left to guard de la Passe. From this advanced post the English were able to communicate with the mainland, and Mr. Farquhar thought he could make an advantageous use of this communication by distributing to the people of the island copies of a proclamation in which the ambition of the French was contrasted disadvantageously with the good government of the English. This somewhat childish demonstration met with the fate that might have been anticipated. It failed to seduce a single islander.

Before adverting to the measures next taken by the English, I propose to remark for a few moments on the state of affairs at this moment in the Isle of France. The Governor of that island was General Count Decäen. He was one of the most distinguished officers of the French Army. He had made his earlier campaigns under Kléber, Hoche, and Moreau. At Hohenlinden he had contributed more than any other general, excepting perhaps General Richepanse, to the decisive victory. Named in 1802 by the First Consul Captain-General of the French possessions to the east of the Cape of Good Hope, he had accompanied Admiral Linois to the Indian waters, had with him visited Pondichery, and recognising the impossibility of keeping that place in the event of the breaking out of a war, then imminent, with England, had sailed to the Isle of France, thence to concert the measures which it might still be possible to direct against the resolute enemy of his country. But he did not stop there. He devoted himself with all the ardour of his generous and enlightened nature to the amelioration of the condition of the islanders. He modified and improved the old commercial laws; he established a number of useful institutions; codified the general, the civil, and the criminal laws of the island, embodying them in a code which, I believe, is still known as the Code Decäen.* So salutary were his reforms, so beneficient was his administration, that many years later an illustrious † Frenchman referring in a speech in the Chamber of Peers to his achievements in the islands, used this remarkable expression: "General Decäen made the people over "whom he ruled almost forget even the names of La "Bourdonnais and of Dupleix."

Such was the man. Let us now glance at the means at his disposal in 1810. He had with him only 800 French troops of the line, ‡ and scattered over the island, from 2000 to 5000 Creole militia. In Port Louis were three frigates, the *Astrée*, the *Vénus*, and *La Manche*: the others, constituting the squadron under Commodore Duperré, had not then returned from their cruise. With these small means to meet a powerful and well-organised attack he must have felt that all the resources, even of his own brave heart, would be abundantly drawn upon.

Before, however, the English had been able to take advantage of the possession of de la Passe Commodore

* So highly appreciated were the merits of this code that when the Isle of France was surrendered to the English, it was made an article of the capitulation that it should be continued to be ruled by the Code Decäen. The article ran: "Shall preserve their religion, laws, and customs."

† Gérard Lacuée Comte de Cessac, one of the ablest of Napoleon's ministers. He died in 1841, leaving behind him, says M. Chanut, "one "of the purest and most honourable reputations of our epoch."

‡ He had also enlisted 500 foreign prisoners, mostly Irish; but these could not be depended upon to fight against their own countrymen.

Duperré returned, bringing with him, besides his own three vessels previously named, two Indiamen, the *Windham* and the *Ceylon*, captured in the Indian waters. As he approached the island on the 20th July, Duperré noticed the Tricolor still flying on the staff of the small fort in the isle de la Passe. With it likewise was a signal advising him that "the enemy was cruising at "the Coin de Mire." A three-masted vessel, also flying the Tricolor, was likewise discerned lying at anchor under the walls of the fort. Deceived by these appearances, Duperré signalled to his squadron to make the best of their way to Grand Port, directing the sloop *Victor* to take the lead closely followed by the *Minerve*, each in passing to communicate with the three-masted vessel lying off de la Passe. The *Victor* sailed on without the smallest suspicion, till, as she was doubling the fort, she received at once broadsides from the strange ship and from the battery on shore; these simultaneously hoisting English colours. The surprise of every one on board the French ships may be conceived. But Duperré was equal to the occasion. Signalling to his ships to keep close to windward, he made his way into the harbour and anchored in a very advantageous position, admitting of constant communication with the shore. In this operation he had, however, the bad fortune to lose one of his prizes, the *Windham*, owing to the indecision displayed by the officer in charge of her.

Notwithstanding the advantageous position taken up by the French commodore, Captain Pym of the *Sirius*, in communication with Captain Willoughby of the *Néréide,* determined to attack him. On the 22nd, accordingly, both these frigates stood in; but they had scarcely arrived within a mile of the enemy's line when the *Sirius* grounded. The *Néréide* did not care to go on alone. The attempt therefore failed for the moment.

Meanwhile intelligence of the events occurring in the vicinity of Grand Port reached General Decäen. That able officer immediately despatched on board Duperré's squadron all the available seamen in the island. He ordered also the three frigates in Port Louis, the *Astrée, La Manche,* and the *Vénus* to proceed under the senior captain, Hamelin,* to the aid of their sisters threatened in Grand Port.

But before Captain Hamelin could reach the scene of action the two English frigates had been reinforced by the *Iphigenia* and the *Magicienne.* As these approached the shoal on which the *Sirius* had struck the previous afternoon, but from which she had just then extricated herself, that vessel and her consort prepared to weigh anchor. But before deciding to renew his attack Captain Pym assembled on board the *Sirius* the captains of the three other ships and all the available pilots. The conference resulted in a resolution to proceed at once to the attack, the certain effect of which no one questioned for a moment.

Duperré had expected this attack; and he had pre-

* Uncle of Admiral Hamelin who commanded the French Black Sea fleet during the Crimean War.

pared to meet it with the skill which marked his long and glorious career. I have said that his ships had easy communication with the shore. All along that shore, below his vessels, he had erected formidable batteries, had armed them with heavy guns, and manned them with those of his sailors who were most skilled in the art of gunnery. His own ships, covered by shoals and by sunken rocks, the navigation amongst which was difficult, had been so placed as to be able to meet with a concentrated fire an advancing enemy. The Indiaman he had taken, the *Ceylon*, had likewise been heavily armed, and the command of her entrusted to one of the best officers at his disposal. Duperré had himself seen to every detail; he had that morning inspected every battery, said a cheery word to every officer, spoken to his captains of his plans and his hopes. Having done this, he waited, with a serene countenance and a bold heart, the advance of the English.

They came on—they too, dauntlessly, even jubilantly. But no sooner had they, sailing close together, arrived within range than the shore batteries opened upon them. The fire was tremendous and effective, but it did not check the onward progress of the British ships. The *Iphigenia*, in accordance with a previously-concerted plan, directed her course towards the *Minerve*, and opened on her so terrible a fire within half pistol-shot that she drove her out of the line. The *Magicienne*, a little ahead of the *Iphigenia*, was about to engage the *Ceylon* when she struck on a hidden rock and lay motionless in the water in such a position that but few of her guns could bear on the enemy. The *Néréide*, close astern of the *Bellone*, commanded by Duperré, engaged that vessel on one side whilst Captain Pym in the *Sirius* attacked her on the other. The French sloop, the *Victor*, was meanwhile doing all in her power to aid the *Minerve* by firing at, and engaging the attention of, the *Iphigenia*.

The number of guns, the weight of metal, the inspiration of attack, all were in favour of the English, and Duperré saw that unless he used his brain to aid the physical power of his men his squadron must be destroyed. He put in force then a manœuvre which he had arranged beforehand in concert with his captains. He signalled to them to cut their cables and let their vessels glide towards the shore. The result fully answered his anticipations. As his own vessel, the *Bellone*, glided slowly towards the shore, Captain Pym, with all the impetuosity of his nature, turned the *Sirius* in pursuit. Not following, however, the exact line the French commodore had taken, he dashed his vessel on to a shoal; and there she remained fixed, immoveable, and powerless.

Having thus rid himself of one enemy, Duperré, ordering his vessels to cast anchor, concentrated all the fire of the *Bellone* on the other, the *Néréide*, which, following the example of the *Sirius*, had likewise drifted on a shoal. Exposed to a most galling fire, the *Néreide* fought until most of her guns were disabled and the greater part of her crew had been killed and wounded. Incapable of protracting the defence she then struck. But in the excitement of the fire and in the blindness of the smoke the hauling down of the Union Jack was not perceived by the enemy, and the French continued their fire for some time longer.*

In the other part of the line, likewise, fortune had inclined to the French. The *Iphigenia,* warned by the fate of her consorts, had warped out of close range. The *Magicienne,* on her rock, had been so pounded by the *Ceylon* and the shore batteries that, when morning broke, she could scarcely keep afloat.

The firing continued all night. At eleven p.m. the crew of the *Magicienne* abandoned her. She blew up immediately afterwards. At the early dawn Duperré sent off a boat's crew to take possession of the *Néréide.* The *Iphigenia* then endeavoured for a short time to extricate the *Sirius* from her position, but failing, that vessel too was abandoned and blown up. Of all the squadron that had sailed so proudly and so confidently to the attack on the previous day the *Iphigenia* alone remained!

But she was not destined to escape. Duperré indeed was unable to get off his stranded ships in sufficient time to follow her to the Isle de la Passe. But just at the opportune moment, just as she had been warped to her station off that islet, there arrived off Grand Port

* Every man on board the *Néréide* was killed or wounded.—*Asiatic Annual Register.*

the squadron of three frigates which General Decäen had despatched from Port Louis. In the presence of a force so overwhelming Captain Lambert of the *Iphigenia* had no alternative but to yield his vessel and the islet. He tried hard to save the former; but General Decäen had arrived at Grand Port, and he dictated terms of absolute surrender. They were with a pang accepted. The *Iphigenia* and her crew were made over to the French, and the Tricolor once more floated over the little fort of the Isle de la Passe.

Thus ended the first attempt of the English on the Isle of France. If we are bound to admire the pluck, the daring, the determination displayed by our countrymen, we cannot, in candour, refuse an equally appreciative acknowledgement of the combined skill and courage by which Duperré converted an apparently certain defeat into a most decisive victory. Later in his career Duperré accomplished great things. In 1814 he defended the lagunes of Venice against an Austrian army; in 1823, at the head of a French squadron, he compelled the surrender of Cadiz; in 1830, commanding a French fleet, he besieged and took Algiers. But it is probable that whenever, during the time intervening between that last great feat of arms and his death in 1846, he might have been disposed to pass in review the events of his distinguished life, he referred with the greatest satisfaction to the repulse and destruction of an English squadron of superior force at Grand Port on the 24th and 25th August, 1810!

Flushed with his success, Decäen resolved to resume the offensive. Collecting all the ships at his disposal, now constituting a formidable squadron, he blockaded the island of Bourbon, intercepting with great success the merchantmen which were bringing supplies to it from India. He hoped to starve the English garrison into submission before it could be strengthened by the large reinforcements which, he well knew, were on their way from India. The only English ship remaining in those waters, the *Boadicea*, 38, had, after the re-capture of the Isle de la Passe, taken refuge in the harbour of St. Paul.

Whilst the blockade of Bourbon was still being maintained the British 38 gun frigate *L'Africaine* appeared off St. Denis (12th September). Captain Rowley instantly brought round the *Boadicea* with the *Otter*, sloop of war, and the *Staunch*, gun-brig, to join the new arrival. The junction having been effected it was resolved to attempt to drive away the blockading force, consisting of the *Iphigénie* * recently captured at Grand Port—and the *Astrée*.

The French frigates stood at once off to sea enticing the enemy to follow them. It was soon found that the *Africaine* was a far better sailer than the French frigates and than her own consort, the *Boadicea*, and that in the chase she was rapidly leaving the latter behind. She therefore shortened sail. Before night fell, however, the *Africaine* had come up close to the enemy, and she

* The French, at once changed the final *a* into *e*.

then endeavoured to maintain this position until day should break, keeping up communication with the *Boadicea* by means of night signals. At three o'clock in the morning, however,—the *Boadicea* being then from four to five miles astern of her consort,—a sudden breeze caught the sails of the *Africaine*, and carried her, not without her commander's consent, within less than musket-shot distance on the weather quarter of the *Astrée*. Captain Corbet, who commanded the English frigate, could not resist the temptation, but at once fired into the enemy. The *Astrée* immediately replied. The second broadside from the *Astrée* severely wounded Captain Corbet, but his place was taken by the first lieutenant, and the action was continued for ten minutes with great spirit. By that time the *Iphigénie* had time to come to the aid of her consort. Whilst the *Astrée* continued within pistol-shot on the larboard beam of the English frigate, the *Iphigénie* came close up on her starboard bow and raked her several times.

A contest so unequal could not long continue. Yet one hour elapsed before the gallant crew of the *Africaine* would confess themselves conquered; and even then it was not till 163 of their number had been killed and wounded.

But the interlude was not yet over. Commodore Rowley of the *Boadicea* noticed at break of day that the *Africaine* had been captured. He did not at once attempt to disturb her conquerors, but made way towards the *Otter* and *Staunch*. Having joined these he set out with them in pursuit of the enemy. The French frigates were not inclined to risk another engagement with three fresh vessels. The rigging of the *Iphigénie* had been so cut up as to render her difficult of management. She had also fired away nearly all her ammunition. Captain Bonnet of the *Astrée* preferred then the abandonment of his prize to an encounter which could scarcely be successful. Taking then, the *Iphigénie* in tow, he abandoned the *Africaine,*—which was helpless,—to her former masters, and returned to Port Louis, capturing on his way a 16-gun cruiser belonging to the East India Company.

Commodore Rowley and his prize then reached the anchorage at St. Paul. The blockade of Bourbon was at the same time resumed by the French frigate *Vénus* 44, and the sloop *Victor*. Whilst engaged in this blockade, these vessels sighted the British 32-gun frigate *Ceylon,* having on board General Abercromby, on his way from Madras to Bourbon, to assume the command of the troops destined to act against the Isle of France. They at once set out in pursuit. The *Vénus,* being a better sailer, soon caught up and engaged the British frigate. After a close contest of three-quarters of an hour, in which the *Vénus* lost her mizen-mast, and the *Ceylon* was rendered almost unmanageable, the *Vénus* assumed a position to leeward, and continued firing only at intervals until the *Victor* * should come up. This

* The *Victor* was no other than our old friend, the *Revenant,* so famous under Surcouf. Taken into the French Navy as the *Jéna,* she

occurred about two hours after the action had begun. The *Victor* then took a raking position athwart the bows of the *Ceylon*, and the latter, then quite helpless, struck her flag.

But there was speedy vengeance in store for the British. The *Boadicea*, accompanied by the *Otter* and *Staunch*, having descried the French frigate with her prize abreast of St. Denis, started off at once in pursuit. The *Victor* vainly endeavoured to take in tow the damaged *Ceylon*, and the latter, cast off, was re-captured. Then came the turn of the *Vénus*. But she had been too much crippled in her fight of the previous night to be able to offer effectual resistance to a fresh and more powerful frigate, and too much damaged in her rigging to escape. Captain Hamelin, who commanded her, made, however, a hot fight of it, and only struck when further resistance had become impossible.*

had been captured by the English and re-named the *Victor*. She was subsequently re-captured by the French.

* It is gratifying to notice the manner in which Hamelin's gallant service, notwithstanding the loss of his ship, was acknowledged by Napoleon. In a despatch from the Minister of Marine, dated 27th December 1810, I find the following:—"His Majesty has remarked with pleasure that you rendered decisive the success which Captain Duperré had obtained between the 23rd and 25th August, and that you subsequently captured the frigate *Ceylon* in a hand-to-hand encounter. Whatever may have been the events which followed, H.M. has not the less appreciated the splendid defence which you made, notwithstanding that, when disabled by a preceding combat, you were attacked by superior forces. He has deigned in appreciation of these different actions, which testify to your courage and to your skill, to promote you to the grade of Commander of the Legion of Honour." The following year Hamelin was created a Baron and promoted to the rank of Rear-Admiral.

The capture of the *Vénus* was the turning point in the scale. Thenceforward the favours of fortune were showered exclusively on the British. Shortly after that event there arrived at St. Denis the frigate *Nisus*, bearing the flag of Vice-Admiral Bertie, the precursor of a fleet and army on their way from England *viâ* the Cape of Good Hope, ordered to co-operate with the troops taken from the three presidencies, and which had started from India about the same time, to effect the reduction of the Isle of France.

VI.

It was not, however, until the 14th October that Admiral Bertie had been able to refit the ships which he found at St. Paul and St. Denis. But on that date he sailed from the former port at the head of the *Boadicea*, the *Africaine*, the *Ceylon*, the *Nisus*, and the *Néréide*,* to blockade Port Louis. Leaving three of these vessels on that duty, he proceeded on the 19th in company with General Abercromby to Rodriguez, there to meet the troops and ships which, coming respectively from England and India, had appointed that little island to be their rendezvous.

On the 24th Admiral Bertie fell in with the British squadron on its way to the Indian seas, commanded by Rear-Admiral Drury and consisting of seven ships. Two of these, the *Cornelia*, 32, and the *Hesper* sloop, were at once sent to increase the blockading force off Port Louis; two others, the *Clorinde*, 38, and the *Doris*, 36, were detained at Rodriguez; the remainder were sent on to their destination. The admiral arrived at Rodriguez on the 3rd November, and found there the

* Formerly the *Vénus*. It will be noticed that three ships of the squadron had been in the possession of the French.

troops which had been sent from Bombay. The division from Madras convoyed by the *Psyche* and *Cornwallis* arrived on the 6th, and that from Bourbon on the 12th November.

The troops from Bengal and those from the Cape were so long in coming, that the admiral, in concert with the general, determined not to wait for them beyond the 21st. All preparations accordingly were made for the expedition to leave Rodriguez on the morning of the 22nd, when, on the evening of the previous day, the happy intelligence was received that the Bengal division was in the offing. The transports conveying it were at once ordered not to drop anchor, but to join the main fleet and accompany it to the selected point of debarkation, Grande Baye, about fifteen miles to the windward of Port Louis.

The armament, independently of the division from the Cape of Good Hope, which did not arrive in time to take any part in the operations, consisted of forty-six transports and a fleet of twenty-one sail.* They carried 11,300 fighting men, composed as follows:—Of regiments of the line there were the 12th, 14th, 22nd, 33rd, 56th, 59th, 65th, 69th, 84th, and 89th regiments; the artillery consisted of four batteries from Bengal and Madras; the European cavalry of one troop of the

* These were the *Illustrious*, 47; the *Cornwallis*, 44; the *Africaine*, the *Boadicea*, the *Nisus*, the *Clorinde*, the *Menelaus*, the *Néréide*, each of 38; the *Phœbe* and *Doris*, of 36; the *Cornelia*, *Psyche*, and *Ceylon*, of 32; the sloops *Hesper*, *Eclipse*, *Hecate*, and *Actæon;* the gun-brig *Staunch*, and four smaller vessels.

26th Dragoons. The native troops from Bengal and Madras consisted of four volunteer battalions and the Madras pioneers; 2000 sailors and marines were likewise contributed by the fleet. The Europeans were to the natives of the force in the proportion of two to one.

General Decäen had not been unconscious of the coming storm. Aware of his own inability to oppose with success any large hostile force led with ordinary prudence, he had nevertheless exerted himself to the utmost to rouse the energies of the colonists. We have seen that he had at his disposal only 800 French troops of the line, in addition to 500 enlisted prisoners, mostly Irish, upon whom he could not depend. The Creole element has been variously estimated. Extravagant English writers have rated it as high as 10,000; but it probably never exceeded 4000; and of these it is recorded by the English annalist of the time,* that "they refused on the approach of the British armament "to co-operate in the defence of the island." A few of the slaves were armed, but in a most cursory and inefficient manner.

General Decäen might, indeed, well have despaired. But he allowed no symptoms of any such feeling, even if he entertained it, to appear. No sooner had he received information that the hostile armament had left Rodriguez than he issued a spirited proclamation†

* *Asiatic Annual Register*, 1101-11.

† The following is a translation of the text of the proclamation:—

"Inhabitants of the Isle of France,—Thirty-four of the enemy's ships calling upon the colonists to aid the army and navy in the defence of the island, promising them victory, should they respond to his call. He could do no more in that way. Then, massing his troops, he took up a position near Port Louis, whence he would be able to move at once upon any threatened point.

Meanwhile the transports carrying the expeditionary force arrived, on the morning of the 29th November, before a narrow passage dividing from the mainland a small island called Gunner's Quoin. It had previously been ascertained by careful survey that this passage offered openings through the reefs by which several boats could enter abreast. Here, then, at ten o'clock in the morning, the fleet came to anchor. The debarkation on the mainland commenced at one p.m., and was conducted to a successful result, without the loss of a single man, in three hours—the small French party which had held Fort Malartic, situated at the head of the bay, retiring on the appearance of the British fleet.

The English army had, previously to its debarkation,

are before the island! This number, which may be increased at any moment, leads us to suppose that the English have not relinquished their intention to attack this colony—an intention in which they have been already once baffled by the glorious success of the brave men of the division of Duperré. I do not forget the proofs of zeal and intrepidity displayed by you both before and after that glorious feat of arms.

"Inhabitants of the Isle of France! In the present conjuncture I would remind you of the enthusiasm with which, on the last anniversary of the fête of the great Napoleon, you renewed your vows of fidelity to your country. You are Frenchmen! Join, then, your valour to the valour of the brave soldiers and marines whom I am about to lead against the enemy, and we shall not fail to be victorious."

been divided into six brigades. The first, under Colonel Picton, was composed of the 12th and 22nd regiments, and the right wing of the Madras volunteer battalion; the second, under Colonel Gibbs, comprised the 59th regiment, 300 men of the 89th and 100 of the 87th formed together as one battalion, and the left wing of the Madras volunteer battalion; the third, under Colonel Kelso, consisted of the 14th regiment and the 2nd Bengal volunteers; the fourth, under Colonel Macleod, was formed of the 69th regiment, 300 marines, and the Madras native flank battalion; the fifth, commanded by Colonel Smith, comprised the 65th regiment, a troop of the 25th Dragoons, and the 1st battalion of the Bengal volunteers; whilst the sixth or reserve brigade, commanded by Lieutenant-Colonel Keating, consisted of a battalion formed of the four flank companies of the 12th and 33rd regiments, of two companies of the 56th, of one of the 14th, one of the 89th, of the 84th regiment, and of Captain Imlack's detachment of Bombay troops which had done such good service in the capture of Bourbon.

The debarkation had no sooner been effected than, leaving the fifth brigade to cover the landing place, General Abercromby, at four o'clock, pushed on with the rest of the force through a very thick wood, lying between the coast and the high road leading to Port Louis. The troops forced their way for fully four miles through an all but impenetrable jungle, entangling their feet at every step, and dragging the guns only by the most untiring exertion. They had, however, the good fortune to debouch into the more open country without any opposition. Just, however, as they reached that more open plain they came upon the advanced picquet of the enemy. The men of the picquet had not evidently anticipated an attack from that quarter, for they were surprised, and, after a faint and irregular fire, they retreated from their position.

Their fire, however, faint and irregular as it was, effected some damage. Two grenadiers were killed, and two officers and several men wounded. Some officers and men likewise succumbed to the intense heat and to the fatigue of the march. The French picquet having retired, General Abercromby encamped his force in the open ground in front of the wood. He resumed his march in the morning with the intention of pushing on to Port Louis. But the heat of the day and the extreme scarcity of water rendered this impossible, and the little army, after marching only five miles, was forced to take up a position for the rest of the day and for the night at Moulin à poudre on the banks of a small river called Pamplemousses, which thus covered the camp.

To return to General Decäen. This officer had anticipated that the English army would disembark at a point nearer to Port Louis—whence the road to the capital was shorter and easier—and he had taken his measures accordingly. He had never imagined that an invader would land his troops on a point where the inland country was covered by an almost impenetrable jungle, defensible by a few determined men against an army. But the moment he received the news brought by the retiring picquet he prepared to meet the new danger—a danger the greater, as the natural defence had been forced and there were but ten miles between the enemy's camp and the capital. It was not, however, until mid-day of the 30th that he was able to collect a force at all respectable to make head against the enemy. This force, consisting—including the Irish prisoners forced into the service—of 1300 Europeans and a few slaves and Creoles, he posted in a rather strong position, about two miles in front of the capital. He drew up his men on a level ground over which the high road passed, the guns in the centre on either side of the road, concealed by brushwood, and both flanks covered by a thick wood, impenetrable on the right and capable of a strong defence on the left. Having so disposed his small force, he galloped forward, followed by his staff, by a few Creole cavalry, and some riflemen, to reconnoitre the English position.

The English had been about two hours in their encampment at Moulin à poudre when General Decäen rode up. Approaching rather too closely, a smart skirmish ensued, in the course of which the French general received a contusion on his leg. What he saw, there, however, was worse than any contusion. He counted a force exceeding his own in the proportion of ten to one, and ready the next morning to cover the five miles which still intervened between it and the capital.

Decäen must have felt as he rode back to his men that, according to the probabilities, further resistance would but cause a useless expenditure of blood. He determined nevertheless to make one effort for victory. On his return to camp he despatched 300 men with two guns to occupy a position commanding the bridge over the Tambeau, about half a mile in front of his camp. Could he but keep the invaders there for a short time he might yet raise a force te operate on their communications.

But it was not to be. Early the following morning, before daylight, General Abercromby detached the fourth brigade to seize the batteries at the Tambeau and Tortue bays, whence it had been arranged that the army was to receive its supplies. The main body of the force, under the personal command of the general, commenced its movement on Port Louis shortly afterwards. After marching about two miles it came within sight of the bridge over the Tambeau. As it was seen to be defended, the advance column was halted, whilst the guns opened with shrapnel on the enemy. The fire was so well directed that the French retired precipitously, leaving uncompleted the destruction—begun and partly executed—of the bridge. They fell back on their main body.

The injury done to the bridge had been so far effectual that the guns of the British were unable to cross it. They had to seek a passage lower down, at a ford commanded by the French artillery. The passage was attended with difficulty and some loss, but was nevertheless accomplished. The British force then moved on the position occupied by the French and flanked by thick woods already described.

General Decäen had witnessed, not unmoved, the passage of the Tambeau. He knew that he was now left with but one card in his hand. He played it boldly. Carefully reserving his fire till the heads of the hostile columns should advance within range, he then opened upon them a concentrated and continuous discharge. This fire, coming from guns which had been masked, checked the advance for a few moments. But it was only that the British troops might deploy. For them there was nothing for it but the bayonet. The advance guard, led by Colonel Campbell of the 33rd, under the general direction of General Ward, having quickly formed, dashed straight on. Nothing could stop their splendid charge. The enemy's troops, after a gallant struggle, in which many of them were killed, were forced back from their position, leaving their guns in the hands of the conquerors. These, however, did not gain a bloodless triumph. Besides several privates, Colonel Campbell, 33rd, and Major O'Keefe, 12th, were killed. Whilst this was going on in the centre an attempt which had been made on the left flank of the French had proved not less successful. After a gallant resistance the enemy's position was forced, and all his guns were taken.*

* In this action the French lost about 100 men, killed and wounded. The return of the English for this engagement, and for the slight

The French force retired across the river Lataniers within the outworks of Port Louis. The English took up a position for the night just beyond cannon-shot of the enemy's lines.

But it was all over. The English fleet commanded the harbour, and the fortifications could not be defended by the small force at the disposal of the Captain-General. Reconnoitring the following morning, General Decäen observed preparations in the enemy's camp, betokening an intention to make a general attack upon the town. Such an attack would, he knew, not only be irresistible, but it would entail upon the inhabitants great calamities. In their interests, then, and in the interests of humanity, having done all that was possible for France, and exhausted every available resource, General Decäen resolved to capitulate. He sent an officer, bearing a flag of truce, with a proposal to this effect to the British camp.

He was just in time. General Abercromby was on the point of despatching a force to the southern side of the town, so that the assault might be combined and general. The proposal for a capitulation alone stopped the movement. The General agreed to it, though demurring to the terms proposed But these were soon arranged. The Isle of France, with all the ships in her harbours, all the arms in her arsenals, all the stores in

encounter in front of the wood on the 29th November, is as follows:—Killed, 28; wounded, 89; missing, 45. Total 162. Besides these one sailor was killed and five were wounded.

her magazines, was transferred bodily to England. One point was insisted on by General Decäen, and, from motives of policy, accorded by the English commander. This was that the French troops should not be considered as prisoners of war, but should be permitted to return to France at the cost of the British Government with their arms and baggage.*

Thus did the French lose, after an occupation of nearly a hundred years, the beautiful island upon which had been bestowed the name of their own bright land, and which in climate, in refinement of luxury, in the love of adventure of its children, had been, in very deed, the France of the East. In the long struggle with England which had followed the Revolution, the Isle of France had inflicted upon the English trade a "damage which "might be computated by millions," whilst she herself had remained uninjured,—for eighteen years indeed—unthreatened. She had proved herself to be that which

* I think it right and fair to give General Abercromby's own reasons for agreeing to the demand of General Decäen in this particular. In his report to Lord Minto he says :—" I was prevailed upon to acquiesce in this indulgence being granted to the enemy, from the desire of sparing the lives of many brave officers and soldiers, and out of regard to the interests of the inhabitants of the island, who have long laboured under the most degrading misery and oppression, added to the late period of the season when every hour became valuable. I considered these to be motives of much more national importance than any injury which would arise from a small body of troops, at so remote a distance from Europe, being permitted to return to their own country free from any engagement." It will be seen that General Abercromby avows that he was influenced solely by considerations of general policy. His statement regarding the misery and oppression of the islanders, of which he had no personal knowledge, may be dismissed as gratuitous.

the Emperor had declared that Cherbourg should become,—"an eye to see and an arm to strike." Protected for long, partly by the storms of the ocean, partly by the daring spirit of her children, partly by the timid counsels of the British Government, she had been, for the privateers who preyed upon the commercial marine of the East India Company, at once a harbour of refuge and a secure base of operation. She had been the terror of British merchants, the spectre which haunted the counting house, the one black spot in the clear blue of the Indian Ocean. The relief which was felt by the merchants of Calcutta was expressed in an address presented by them to Lord Minto, in which they offered their "sincere congratulations on the capture of the "only remaining French colony in the East, which has "for so many years past been the source of devastation "to the commerce of India, to a magnitude almost "exceeding belief."*

The ease with which the Isle of France was captured in 1810 suggests the question why she was so long allowed to pursue her aggressive career? An investigation of the cause of this apathy on the part of the British, when so many interests were at stake, can only

* It may interest many of those now residing in Calcutta to read the names of the merchants who signed this address. They were—Alexander Colvin, John Palmer, J. D. Alexander, J. H. Fergusson, Robert Downie, James Mactaggart, Joseph Barretto, John Robertson, James Scott, Johannes Sarkies and William Hollings. The object of the address was to ask Lord Minto to sit for his portrait in commemoration of the capture of the isle.

tend to confirm the conviction of the prescience and wisdom of Marquess Wellesley, to show very clearly the unsoundness of the timid policy by which he was so often overruled. The great Marquess not only urged an exepdition in 1800; he fitted one out in 1801. This was diverted to Egypt. Shortly afterwards the Court of Directors, dreading the genius which would, if unfettered, have advanced the civilisation of India by twenty years, replaced him by a Governor-General who began by undoing the large work of unification which his predecessor had initiated. When Lord Cornwallis died, the Court of Directors, after vainly endeavouring to confer the Governor-Generalship on a narrow-minded reactionist—who, in the short term of his acting incumbency, confirmed and extended a system which left the states of Ríjpútáná a prey to Maráthá freebooters,—imposed a policy upon Lord Minto which restricted his power for that kind of aggressive warfare which is so often the best and surest defence. It is a high testimony to Lord Minto's intellect that in the end he burst those trammels, and forced one portion, at least, of the policy of Marquess Wellesley on a peace-loving Court of Directors and a distrusting ministry.

It was Lord Minto then who, taking up the dropped thread of the policy of Marquess Wellesley, wrested the Isle of France from her parent country. For France indeed, even her name, the name she had borne for about a hundred years, perished on the 3rd December 1810. Called by her discoverers, the Portuguese, Cerné;

re-named in 1598 by the Dutch after their Maurice of Nassau, Mauritius; falling, after her abandonment by the Dutch between 1703 and 1710, into the possession of the French, the island had been subsequently known to the world by the name she bore when the English captured her. But the name did not suit the new conqueror. It was erased, and that bestowed in honour of the great Stadtholder was substituted. The Isle of France vanished from history with the last month of the year 1810!

With her conquest, too, ended the careers of the privateers on the Indian seas. They, too, vanished with the island which had nurtured them. Thenceforward the huge Indiamen of the Company could sail in comparative safety. In the course of a few years not only did the dread of the French cruisers vanish, but their exploits came to be listened to with a smile. Not the less, however, are the deeds which they did accomplish worthy of being recorded. They show that if, in a future war, privateering should again be legitimatized, it may be possible for a nation whose navy shall have been annihilated and whose ports shall be blockaded, to inflict, by means of it, on a nation which may even bear the title of the mistress of the seas, losses the full extent of which it would be almost impossible to estimate.

BOOK III.

FOREIGN ADVENTURERS IN INDIA.

After the failures of the direct attempts made by Dupleix, by Lally, and by Suffren to establish French domination in Southern India, there remained to the Latin race but one mode of counteracting the progress of the English. That mode may be described in a few words. To enable the princes of India to meet the English successfully in the field it was necessary above all things to impart to their troops a thorough knowledge of European discipline and a complete acquaintance with the system of European strategy. To this somewhat venturesome task the sons of France bent themselves with untiring energy. They gave to it often their lives, almost always their every faculty. They had much to aid them. The native princes who employed them knew at least that their hatred of England was not feigned; that they had nothing so much at heart as the humiliation of the rival of their own country. They therefore gave them, almost always, a confidence without stint. Their behests were but rarely refused. They worked under the avowed sanction and with the authority of the prince whom they served. And if they did not succeed, their want of success is to be attributed rather to the jealousies which prevented combination amongst the native princes, than to any shortcomings on the part of the ablest and most influential amongst them.

Of all these adventurers de Boigne was, with one exception, the ablest and the most successful. Born at Chambéry, the 8th March, 1751, the son of a furrier, Benoit de Boigne was at an early age sent to study law at the College of his native town. But he had scarcely attained the age of seventeen when his adventurous nature impelled him to renounce his studies, and to seek excitement in a career of arms. In 1768, then, he entered the regiment of Clare, a regiment in the Irish Brigade in the service of France, and then commanded, in the absence of Lord Clare, by Colonel Leigh. De Boigne joined the regiment with the rank of ensign at Landrecies, and applied all the ardour of his youth to master the science of his profession. In this task he received great encouragement and assistance from Colonel Leigh, and, under his tuition, de Boigne attained a complete knowledge of the art of war as it was understood in those days.

After serving in garrison for three years and a half at Landrecies, the regiment of Clare was ordered to Dunkerque to embark for the Isle of France. The regiment, having taken its tour of duty in the island for eighteen months, returned to France, and, disembarking at L'Orient, was ordered to Béthune.

This happened in 1773. France was then at peace with all the world, and no prospect of war seemed to loom in the future. The promotion of de Boigne had been slow, and, beginning to feel disgusted with a life so monotonous and so devoid of enterprise, he asked himself if it would not be advisable to seek another scene for the occupation of the abilities he felt that he possessed. It chanced that Russia was then at war with Turkey. The Russian Government was in the habit in those days of welcoming eagerly instructed officers into the ranks of its army. De Boigne resolved, then, to resign his commission in the French service and to offer himself to her northern ally.

His resignation was accepted, and de Boigne went to Turin. Obtaining there letters of introduction to Count Orloff, who commanded the Russian land and sea forces in the Grecian Archipelago, he returned to Marseilles and embarked on board the first ship sailing thence for Greece. Almost immediately on his arrival there he was appointed captain in a Greek regiment in the service of the Empress Catherine. This regiment formed a part of the army employed in besieging the island of Tenedos. A detachment of it, to which de Boigne belonged, having been sent to effect a descent on that island, the Turks made a sortie, attacked the invaders in great force, and cut them off nearly to a man. De Boigne escaped with his life, but was taken prisoner and sent first to Chio and thence to Constantinople.

Seven months later the war came to an end, and de Boigne, with the other prisoners of war, was released. He had then attained the rank of major in the Russian army. Peace, however, had closed for him the avenues of further advancement. De Boigne then quitted the Russian service and embarked for Smyrna. Meeting in that town some Englishmen who had returned from India, he was so struck by their description of the adventurous life of that country, that he resolved to seek his fortune there. Returning to Constantinople, he made his way to Aleppo, and joined there a caravan just setting out for Basrá. The caravan reached Bagdad in safety, but, as a furious war was then raging between the Turks and the Persians, the road thence to Basrá was deemed too dangerous to be traversed, and the caravan returned to Aleppo.

From that place de Boigne made his way as quickly as he could back to Smyrna and sailed thence to Alexandria. In his journey from Alexandria to Rosetta he was shipwrecked and fell into the hands of the Arabs. These, with characteristic hospitality towards a stranger, befriended him, and by their aid he was able to reach Cairo. Here innumerable delays occurred, and it was owing to the kindness of the English consul, Mr. Baldwin, that means were at last provided for him to reach India. He embarked at Suez and sailed thence at the end of the year 1777 for Madras.

Amongst those whom de Boigne had met in his European wanderings was an English nobleman, Earl Percy. With him he had formed a friendship, and Lord Percy had in consequence furnished him with letters to Lord Macartney and to Warren Hastings. On his arrival at Madras, de Boigne wished at first to act independently of the British Government. But the circumstances of the time were against him. The British were on the eve of their last war with Haidar Ali, and it is natural to suppose that they should be unwilling to afford opportunities for foreign adventurers to find their way to the camp of that formidable leader. Having no other resource, then, de Boigne, who had been a major in the Russian service, accepted the rank of ensign in the 6th regiment Madras Native Infantry.

The war broke out immediately afterwards. It happened that the 6th regiment N. I. was one of those under the command of Colonel Baillie when that officer was attacked by the combined forces of Haidar and Tippú at Perambákam in September, 1780. A few days before that fatal conflict, however, two companies of the 6th regiment had been sent to escort supplies of grain to the main army. With these two companies was de Boigne, and in this manner he escaped the almost entire destruction which befell the main body of his regiment.

Shortly after this de Boigne quitted the English service. Various reasons have been assigned for this step.* But he himself undoubtedly stated the truth when he affirmed that in a service of progressive promotion there was, at his age, no chance of his ever attaining to high command. He resolved, therefore, to return to Europe by way of Káshmir, Afghánistán, and Persia.

With this object in view he came round to Calcutta and presented to Warren Hastings Lord Percy's letter and one with which he had been provided by Lord Macartney. That illustrious statesman gave him a warm and cordial reception; entirely approved of his design to return to Europe by the route he had indicated; and furnished him with letters to the British residents at the various native courts he would be likely to visit *en route*, as well as to the independent native princes in alliance with the British Government.

At Lakhnao, the first city which he visited on his travels, de Boigne was extremely well received by the Nawáb, to whom he had been presented by the resident. Not only was a khilat of the value of 4000 rupees bestowed upon him, but the Nawáb presented him likewise with a bill on the bankers of Kábal for 6000 rupees, and another for an equal amount on those of Kándahár. At Lakhnao de Boigne remained

* *Vide* Ferdinand Smith's Sketch, pages 67-68; the Article de Boigne in the *Nouvelle Biographie Générale;* and the *Memoire sur la carrière du Général Comte de Boigne.*

five months, making many friends amongst the English officers and studying their system. He then went on to Delhi where he arrived at the end of the month of August.

The Emperor of Delhi at that time was Shah Alam; his minister, Mirza Shaffi. Without the aid of the latter it was impossible for de Boigne to obtain an interview with the Emperor, and Mirza Shaffi was in the camp before Agra. Thither, accordingly, de Boigne repaired.

It was during his sojourn in this camp that de Boigne's ideas took a direction which influenced his whole life. Rebuffed by the minister, who refused to allow him to be presented to Shah Alam, he turned his attention to the political events passing before his eyes. Noting the rivalry of the various native princes, the indiscipline of their armies, the ignorance and want of knowledge of their generals, it occurred to him that a great career was open to an instructed European soldier. The unleavened masses were fermenting all about him. Let the instructed European soldier but procure for himself the authority to leaven but one of those masses, and his master would become the chief of all his rivals, if not indeed the ruler of India. The idea grew daily; it ripened quickly into feasibility; thenceforth the career of de Boigne was determined.

At that time the Ráná of Góhad was closely besieged in his fort by Mádhají Sindia. To offer himself to the latter, immensely superior in power to the Ráná, would have been a folly. In such a case, even had Mádhají accepted his services, no credit to himself could possibly have resulted. But to enter the service of the besieged Ráná, and by skill and dexterity to paralyse the movements of his enemy, would be to gain a reputation and to acquire a moral power such as would open out the brightest prospects for the future. Thus reasoning, de Boigne made secretly the following proposition to the Ráná. He offered, in consideration of a certain stipulated sum of money, to raise 2000 men at Agra, 1000 at Jaipúr, 4000 at Delhi, and 1000 near Góhad; to concentrate these troops with all imaginable secrecy at a point on the frontier of the Ráná's territory; and with them to attack the besieging force in the rear, and drive it from his dominions.

The Ráná of Góhad, without declining this offer, did not at once accept it. He hoped rather to be rescued from his perilous condition by the intervention of the English. Meanwhile, however, he was not sufficiently careful to keep the secret. With the publicity he allowed to be imparted to the offer, the possibility of carrying it into execution vanished. De Boigne then broke off the negotiation, and offered his services to the Rájá of Jaipúr.

But before an answer could come from Jaipúr, de Boigne had accepted an invitation from Mr. Anderson, the British resident at the court of Mádhají, to visit him in the camp. Mádhají Sindia was then besieging Gwáliár. Thither accordingly de Boigne repaired, and there he agreed to remain, the guest of Mr. Anderson, until he should receive the reply of the Rájá.

De Boigne received that reply at the end of October (1783). His offer was accepted. Before taking up the appointment, however, he thought it becoming to inform Warren Hastings officially of his intention to renounce his journey to Europe and to take service with the Rájá of Jaipúr. Warren Hastings, in reply, requested de Boigne to return in the first instance to Calcutta that he might inform him personally of the sentiments entertained by the government of India regarding the course he proposed to pursue. De Boigne, though sensible of the arbitrary nature of this request, felt that his gratitude and his interest alike counselled him to comply with it. He returned accordingly to Calcutta,—no easy journey in those days. On his arrival there Warren Hastings informed him that his requisition had been necessary because he, de Boigne, had given an official form to his letter, and that as such it had been laid before the council; that as Governor-General in Council he could not give him authority to enter the service of a native prince, although, in his private capacity, he had no objection to his following such a course, and that if he chose to follow it, he would shut his eyes to his proceedings. The Governor-General added that he was about to set out for Lakhnao, and that he hoped de Boigne would accompany him so far.

Armed with this power to act as he might think best, de Boigne accompanied the Governor-General to

Lakhnao, hastened thence to Agra, and obtaining there a small escort, pushed on towards Jaipúr. The difficulties, and they were not slight, which he encountered in his journey were surmounted, and in the spring of 1784 he reached Jaipúr.

But here disappointment awaited him. In the long interval which had elapsed between the acceptance of his offer and his arrival, the Jaipúr policy had changed. Peaceful councils now prevailed, and the Rájá had no need of a general. To compensate de Boigne, however, for the trouble and expense which had been caused him the Rájá presented him with 10,000 rupees.

Disappointed though not daunted, de Boigne repaired to Dehli. At this time the murder of Mirza Shaffi and the anarchy which had followed, had reawakened in the mind of Mádhají Sindia the hope of becoming master of the capital of the Moghols. He was fully sensible of the new difficulties which the power he might thus acquire would cause him: but, being able, farsighted, and ambitious, he was nursing his resources and seeking for means to meet the crisis which might arrive at any moment. At the time of de Boigne's arrival Sindia was in the vicinity of Agra, organising an expedition against Bandalkhand.

For this expedition de Boigne offered his services. He proposed to raise two regiments, each 850 strong; and to equip and organise them in the European fashion.

Mádhají knew de Boigne by reputation, and by something more. The offer he had made to the Ráná of Góhad had struck him at the time as betokening a daring and resolute nature; and, subsequently, when de Boigne had passed a night in his camp on his way to join Mr. Anderson, Mádhají caused his tent to be pillaged. The property then taken was restored but the papers were retained. It is probable that a perusal of these confirmed the impression which the Góhad scheme had given birth to. Such a man, he thought, could scarcely fail to be an acquisition. He accepted, then, after a short delay, de Boigne's offer.

The terms agreed to by de Boigne were that he should receive 1000 rupees a month for himself, and eight rupees a month for each man, officers and privates indiscriminately. To enable himself to give a proper salary to the officers, de Boigne fixed the pay of the privates at rupees 5-8-0 each. This arrangement provided him with 4250 rupees monthly for the officers.

The men were speedily raised; but the drilling was a matter of more difficulty. De Boigne had resolved to teach them European drill, to arm them with European weapons, and to impart to them European discipline. "The labour which this imposed on an individual," writes Mr. Grant Duff, "can easily be conceived by any "person acquainted with military affairs." It was, indeed, at the outset a task which required no ordinary patience, perseverance, and self-control. But at length he had the satisfaction of seeing the end attained. Five months after he had enlisted his men, he marched with two perfectly disciplined regiments to join in Bandalkhand the army commanded by Appa Khandé Ráo.

In the short campaign which followed, the two battalions under de Boigne constituted the entire infantry of the Maráthá army, the remainder being mainly cavalry and a few guns. As it was a campaign of sieges the brunt of the work fell, naturally, on his newly raised troops; and this work they performed with valour and with success. In the midst of his triumphs, however, de Boigne was called away to join the main army of Mádhají at Dehli.

On the 22nd October 1784 the prime minister of the Emperor Shah Alam, Afrasiáb Khan, was murdered by the brother of the minister whose assassination he had instigated. In the terror that followed this murder all parties turned to Mádhají. The Emperor invested him with a power virtually supreme. By his advice the Péshwa was nominated Wakil-úl-Mútlúk or Supreme Deputy of the Empire, Mádhají was appointed Deputy of the Péshwa, Commander-in-chief of the Moghol armies, and the provinces of Agra and Dehli were confided to his management.

But Mádhají was not too elated by his success. He was well aware that the power which had been conferred by acclamation in a time of terror, of difficulty, and of danger, would be disputed as soon as men's minds should begin to calm. He therefore took instant measures to strengthen his position, and amongst other precautions he summoned de Boigne and his battalions from Bandalkhand.

To describe fully the events which followed could only be effected by trenching upon ground already occupied.* I must be satisfied with referring, as briefly as may be, to the deeds of de Boigne himself. Thus, in May 1787, he fought at Lálsót for three days under the eyes of Mádhají against the Patáns and Rájpúts, and when, on the third, the other infantry of Sindia's army, 14,000 in number, deserted to the enemy, de Boigne kept his men true to their colours. For eight consecutive days they continued, as they retreated, to repulse the enemy's attacks. At the battle of Chaksána, fought on the 24th April 1788 against the same enemies, Sindia confided the command of his right wing to a Frenchman, M. Lesteneau, and of his left to de Boigne, whilst the centre was commanded by a native, Sindia being in reserve with the cavalry. On this occasion de Boigne and Lesteneau not only repulsed the attacks made on their wings, but were prepared to render the victory decisive had they been supported by the centre and the cavalry. But no prayers could induce either to advance, and the action, undecided, terminated by a retreat from the field. A few weeks later, however, an ample revenge was taken for these checks. On the 18th June, in the battle fought before Agra, the battalions of de Boigne

* Keene's *Fall of the Moghol Empire*, a vivid and accurate account of the event in Hindostan from the death of Aurangzib to the beginning of the present century.

and their leader contributed greatly to the victory obtained over the Patán chief. Less than four months later, de Boigne's battalions and the bulk of the Maráthá army re-occupied Dehli. Mádhají himself followed shortly after.

The splendid service rendered by the two battalions of de Boigne at Lálsót, at Agra, and at Chaksána, their fidelity when their irregular comrades had deserted, and their unvarying steadiness under fire, had particularly attracted the notice of Mádhají Sindia. But the prejudices of the Maráthá were still strong within him. When, therefore, de Boigne pointed out to him that these two battalions, though perfectly efficient, and capable even of retarding a defeat, were yet insufficient to decide the fortunes of a campaign; that it would be advisable to increase them to the strength of a *corps d'armée*, with artillery attached, Mádhají hesitated. Influenced partly, probably, by a dread to place in the hands of a European a small army obedient only to the orders of its immediate general; partly by the Maráthá leaning towards cavalry, partly also by the annihilation of his enemies and by the expense which the proposed scheme would entail, Mádhají resolved to defer his sanction. As, however, he indicated no fixed time for the announcement of a final decision, de Boigne regarded his reply as a veiled refusal. He therefore offered his resignation. Mádhají accepted it.

De Boigne left Dehli a comparatively rich man. It is stated that he owed the greater part of his wealth to the munificence of Mádhají, who thus showed his gratitude for the unequalled services rendered to him during the late campaigns. Certain it is that, renouncing his military career, he proceeded to Lakhnao, and there on the advice of his old friend, Claude Martin, engaged in mercantile speculations which speedily augmented his capital. He was still engaged in these when he received from Mádhají pressing solicitations to re-enter his service, accompanied by an assurance that he would be at liberty to carry out the measures he had formerly proposed.

The fact was that Mádhají Sindia had not found his position by any means so assured as, in the first moment of his triumph, it had appeared to him. The Patán army had been beaten and dispersed, but its soldiers still existed. He was menaced from the north by the Afgháns, from the west by the Rájpúts, whilst he had perhaps even more to dread from the jealousy of Náná Farnawís, the minister of the Péshwa, and from the scarcely veiled hostility of the other chiefs of the Maráthás.

He felt the want, then, of just such a body of troops as de Boigne had proposed to raise,—troops who would surpass all his other troops in skill and discipline; who would obey one man, and that man impervious to intrigue, devoted to himself alone. In this extremity he bethought him of de Boigne: and upon that thought there speedily followed the missive of which I have spoken.

De Boigne was not deaf to the demand. Arranging,

as speedily as was possible, his commercial affairs, which, however, he left in full action in the hands of agents, he hastened to Mathurá, where Mádhají then had his head quarters. His proposals were at once agreed to. He was authorised to raise a *corps d'armée* consisting of thirteen battalions of infantry, of 500 cavalry, and of sixty guns.

De Boigne went to his task with his accustomed energy. He reclaimed the two battalions he had drilled and commanded before. A third battalion was formed of the soldiers who had been raised and drilled by the Frenchman, Lesteneau, but who, mutinying for arrears of pay, had, on the advice of de Boigne, been disbanded. He had to enlist men from Rohilkhand and Oudh for seven more battalions. All these were dressed and drilled on the European principle. But, in addition to these ten battalions, de Boigne raised three more of Afgháns, dressed in their national costume, and armed with matchlocks and bayonets. For the service of the camp he raised 500 Méwátis, dressed and armed as irregular troops.

The *corps d'armée* thus consisted of 8500 regular infantry, 2400 Afgháns, 500 Méwátis, 500 cavalry, and 100 artillerymen. Each regiment was commanded by a European officer. These officers were men of all nations, many of them British, and in many instances respectable by birth, education, and character.* There were always

* Grant Duff, vol. iii., chapter ii. Subsequently the number of men in each regiment was fixed at 700.

two European officers to each regiment, sometimes more. The non-commissioned officers were in the first instance taken from the three disciplined battalions. The colours of the corps were the national flag, the white cross, of Savoy.

For its command de Boigne was granted a salary of 4000 rupees a month. To provide for this, as well as for the regular payment of the troops, Mádhají made over assignments of land to the charge and management of de Boigne, allowing him two per cent. upon the net revenue, in addition to his regular pay.*

By dint of great exertions the new *corps d'armée* was brought into a condition fitting it for active service early in the year 1790. An opportunity soon offered for the display of its efficiency. On the 20th June the Maráthá army engaged, near Patán, the Patáns under Ishmael Beg, aided by the Rájpút troops of Jaipúr and Jódhpúr. The battle was obstinate and bloody. Holkar, who had promised to aid Mádhají, held aloof. The Patáns three times charged through the infantry of de Boigne, cutting down the artillerymen at their guns. But the coolness of de Boigne and the discipline of his troops soon repaired this disaster. With re-serried ranks they attacked the too daring enemy and drove him back. Then there opened on both sides a heavy artillery fire. This ceasing on the part of the Maráthás at six o'clock in the evening, de Boigne placed himself at the head of his infantry and led them to the charge.

* Grant Duff, vol. iii., chapter ii.

The attack was irresistible. One by one the hostile positions were carried. At nine o'clock the enemy were in complete flight, utterly disorganised, having lost all their guns—ten battalions of their infantry having previously surrendered.

De Boigne then received orders to invade Jódhpúr. He proceeded at once to the siege of Ajmír, but learning that the Rájpúts had assembled a considerable army at Mírtá, he left about 2700 men to blockade Ajmír and started to attack the enemy.

At daybreak on the 12th September, de Boigne assailed the enemy's position. By nine o'clock he had obtained a complete victory. He gained this victory notwithstanding a false movement made by one of his lieutenants, and which for a time left his right wing exposed to the incessant charges of the Rahtór cavalry. The Savoyard, however, showed himself quite equal to the occasion. At nine o'clock, as I have said, the Rájpúts were beaten; at ten o'clock their camp and all their guns and baggage were captured; at three p.m., the town of Mírtá was taken by assault. Peace followed this decisive victory.

Sindia had now satisfied himself as to the immense advantage he had derived from possessing a *corps d'armée* armed and disciplined on the European principle—and commanded by a de Boigne. The troops thus disciplined and thus organised had disposed of his Mahomedan and Rájpút enemies, but he still looked for more at their hands. It must never be lost sight of that the great dream of Mádhají Sindia's life was to unite all the native powers of India in one great confederacy against the English. In this respect he was the most farsighted statesman that India has ever produced. But to bring about this great end it was necessary that, in addition to the power which he wielded at Dehli and in a part of central India, he should be master of all the resources of the Maráthá empire. This he felt would be impossible until he could rid the Péshwa of the minister, Náná Farnawis, who was jealous of his reputation. Nor, he felt, could this end be obtained unless he could dispose of Holkar, the agent and last hope of the Náná. His plan, then, was to crush Holkar, to proceed to Púna, and, obtaining then from the Péshwa the requisite authority, to unite all India in a crusade against the English. It was a grand idea, one capable of realisation by Mádhají, but by him alone, and which, but for his death, would have been realised.

Full of these views, and preparing carefully for the conflict he saw looming in the future, Mádhají determined at this time to increase still further the force which had been so useful to him. De Boigne was authorised to increase it to 18,000 regular infantry, 6000 irregulars, 2000 irregular horse, 600 Afghán cavalry, and 2000 guns. The force thus raised was to be divided into three brigades, or, as it would be more proper to call them, divisions. For their payment a tract of country between Mathurá and Dehli and some lands east of the Jamna, comprising in all fifty-two districts, yielding ultimately twenty-two lakhs of rupees, were assigned to de Boigne. That general was authorised to reserve to himself two per cent. of that revenue, in addition to his pay, now increased to 6000 rupees a month,—a sum which was doubled by other duly authorised emoluments. The fortress at Agra was assigned to him as a depôt of small arms and cannon. Over these fifty-two districts de Boigne was assigned, by Sindia, a power in civil and military matters entirely absolute. He fixed his headquarters at Aligarh.

It was while de Boigne was raising and drilling his brigades, casting guns, and bringing the districts under his sway into order; whilst Mádhají Sindia was endeavouring to arrange the scheme which was the dream of his later years, that war broke out between the British and Tippú Súltán. This war was a blow to Mádhají. He disapproved this isolated attack upon a power to which united India might only possibly be a match. Still more was he annoyed and enraged at finding that the Péshwa, guided by Náná Farnawis, had entered into an alliance with the common enemy. Nothing, Mádhají had always felt, could be more noxious to the general cause of the native princes of India, than the union of one chief with their most formidable rival to put down another chief. Still, for the moment, he was powerless to prevent this fatal action. He was forced to content himself with husbanding his resources, with guarding against an attack from the north, and with preparing his army for the great event to which he looked forward. Having done all that was possible in this respect, he set out for Púna, determined, after repressing Holkar, and unseating Náná Farnawis, to obtain the chief power himself, and, wielding it, to make one supreme effort to drive the British from Hindostan.

Mádhají left de Boigne and the greater part of his *corps d'armée* behind. He took with him as escort only two battalions, commanded by Hessing and Filoze. He arrived at Púna the 11th June, 1793.

Scarcely, however, had Mádhají crossed the borders of his own territories than his enemies began to raise their heads. First, the widow of Najíf Khan, a former prime minister at the Imperial Court of Dehli, refused to surrender the fort of Kanúnd to Sindia's officers. De Boigne sent one of his brigades, under the orders of M. Perron, to compel her. The often-defeated Ishmail Beg raised troops to support her. He encountered Perron under the walls of Kanúnd, and though beaten, yet succeeded in penetrating into the fort with a considerable body of men. The defence was prolonged in consequence, but, the widow having been killed, Ishmail Beg, distrusting the garrison, surrendered himself and the fort to the French leader.

But this was not all. Taking advantage of the absence of Mádhají, Túkají Holkar, the minister of the famous Ahalya Bae, suddenly crossed the river Chambal in great force, and marched towards Rájpútáná, pretending that the aggressions of Mádhají's agent, Gopál Ráo Bháo, forced him to this act of open hostility.

Gopál Ráo Bháo had but a small force under him in Rájpútáná. Aware that Túkají was supported by a body of native troops, armed and drilled in the European fashion, and commanded by the Chevalier Dudrenec, Gopál Ráo sent pressing messages to de Boigne, and to Lakhwa Dádá, commanding the main body of Sindia's cavalry, to join him without delay. De Boigne set out at once from Aligarh at the head of 9000 infantry, and joined Gopál Ráo before the latter had been molested by Holkar. Lakhwa Dádá brought in his cavalry at the same time. De Boigne immediately assumed command of the combined force, consisting of 9000 infantry, 20,000 cavalry, and about forty guns, and forthwith marched upon the enemy. Túkají became now aware of the double mistake he had committed; in the first place, in becoming the aggressor; in the second, in not at once crushing the small force opposed to him. He did his utmost, then, to avoid a general engagement. But de Boigne was not to be denied. He followed him up vigorously, and at last, on the 20th September, had the satisfaction of finding himself in front of his enemy posted at the pass of Lakhairí on the road leading from Kanúnd to Ajmír.

Túkají and Dudrenec had under them four battalions of sepoys, trained by Dudrenec, about 30,000 irregulars, mostly cavalry, and thirty-eight guns. The position they occupied was very formidable. The pass of Lakhairí was extremely narrow; covered in front by wet ground, and impossible to be turned, both flanks being guarded by thick woods and rising ground.

De Boigne felt as he reconnoitred this strong position that he would have to deploy all his resources. Yet his own position was not without some considerable countervailing advantages. His men were covered by tangled forests, impervious to cavalry. His attack might fail, yet his position could not be forced. All other things being equal, victory must incline, he saw, to the side which possessed the greatest number of steady infantry. That side was his own.

There was nothing for it but to move straight on. He placed himself accordingly at the head of his tried battalions and batteries, and ordered them to advance. No sooner, however, did they emerge from the forest than the enemy's artillery opened a tremendous and effective fire upon them. De Boigne continued, however, to advance, and his own guns were soon sufficiently clear of the jungle to take up a position and reply. But they had scarcely fired half a dozen rounds before an event happened which might have been fatal in its consequences. The fire from the enemy's guns caused the explosion first of one tumbril and then immediately afterwards of twelve others continguous to it. The effect might have been made decisive. Túkají at once launched forth his cavalry to make it so. But De Boigne was equal to the occasion. He caused his men to fall back rapidly into the jungle. They reached it, before Túkají's cavalry, feebly handled, could attack them. A concentrated fire of musketry sent back the horsemen more rapidly than they had advanced. A charge from Sindia's cavalry completed their overthrow. Thenceforward they took no part in the contest.

The cavalry having disappeared, de Boigne once more advanced his infantry and his guns. This time there was no mistake. The pass was so narrow that not more than three columns could act abreast. Covering these with 500 Rohilla skirimishers he crossed the wet ground and charged. But the battalions of Dudrenec did not give ground. They stood, and fought, and died at their post. But they were as one to three. The greatest number must inevitably prevail. And it happened so. After the most desperate conflict he had ever been engaged in, the troops of de Boigne stood the victors on the summit of that fatal pass! There was not a man to be pursued. The enemy's cavalry had disappeared, his infantry had died fighting; the guns had been captured!

This victory broke for a time the power of Holkar and left Mádhají undisputed master of the situation. De Boigne followed it up by marching against the Rájá of Jaipúr who had shown a disposition to take advantage of Holkar's outburst. De Boigne's movements were so rapid and his plans so well laid that the Rájá was glad to compromise by submission, based on the payment of his arrears of tribute, and an immediate sum of seventy lakhs of rupees. De Boigne then returned to Aligarh, marching by Alwar, the Rájá of which place had some years before displayed great loyalty to Sindia in very critical circumstances. Here he had an audience of the Rájá. An incident which occurred at this audience is thus related in de Boigne's memoirs. "One day when "the Rájá gave audience to the general, whom he had "made to sit near him, M. de Boigne observed the "minister of the Rájá, who was standing behind his "master, bend down and whisper into his ear some "words in the Persian language—a language which the "general did not understand. The Prince replied only "by a sign of disapproval and by a look in which anger "and indignation were painted. The general's vakil "turned pale. The conversation nevertheless continued "as before, and the audience terminated without the "general having conceived the least suspicion. But in "going out of the palace he was informed by his vakil— "who knew Persian, and who had overheard the words "whispered by the minister—that the latter had proposed "to the Rájá to assassinate de Boigne in the hall of "audience." De Boigne took no notice of the incident.

The power of Mádhají Sindia was now consolidated in Hindostan. While his armies had been triumphing in Rájpútáná his policy had been gaining ground at Púna, whither, on his request, de Boigne had expedited 10,000 of his trained infantry under the command of Perron. Mádhají, in fact, was on the point of crossing the threshold to attain which had been the dream of his later years. His plans had been successful everywhere; and he was on the eve of gaining the pinnacle which would have enabled him to form one vast combination against the English, when he was attacked by fever and died (12th February, 1794).

With him the fabric raised with so much patience, so much skill, and so much foresight, fell to the ground. His successor, Daolat Ráo, was a boy of fifteen, with a character which, if unformed, still showed the germs of waywardness and of a want of self-control.

At the time of Mádhají's death de Boigne was virtually governor of Hindostan. Daolat Ráo confirmed him in this appointment, and he held it, resisting the advances made him by the partisans of the blind Emperor, Shah Alim, till the end of 1795. In the interval, feeling his health weakened, he had more than once asked permission to resign; but Daolat Ráo had as often begged him to remain. At last, at the end of 1794, he yielded to his urgent solicitations, and granted him permission to leave for Europe, still retaining him in his service.

De Boigne bade farewell to the officers of his army in February 1796, and set out for Calcutta. He took with him the regiment of cavalry which was his own peculiar property. He had offered this regiment to Sindia, but Daolat Ráo proposed to pay for it only on the return of de Boigne to India. On his way through Lakhnao he offered it to the Nawáb, but they could not agree as to the terms. Finally he offered it to the English government; Lord Cornwallis took it on the general's own conditions. These were 500 rupees for each horse, or for the entire corps, consisting of 600 horses, 100 camels, four pieces of light artillery, and some draught cattle, 360,000 rupees. The men at the same time entered the British service.

De Boigne embarked for Europe in September 1796, and arrived in London in January, 1797. There he married Mademoiselle d'Osmond, daughter of the Marquis d'Osmond. The marriage, however, was not happy. He remained principally in England during the Empire, but shortly after its fall he settled at the Villa Buisson near Chambéry. He spent the last years of his life in making a philanthropic use of the enormous fortune he had acquired. In Chambéry itself he built a theatre, and a college for the Jesuits, and embellished the town by new and handsome streets. When he died on the 21st June 1830, he left 1,200,000 francs to build a hospital for old men; 500,000 for a hospital for the insane; 300,000 for the permanent relief of beggars; 200,000 francs for new beds in other hospitals, and 100,000 francs for the education of young girls. To his wife he left a life income of 600,000 francs.

It is impossible to part with de Boigne without adding some details regarding his person, his character, and his mode of administration. The following somewhat prolix description was written by a contemporary, one who knew him personally, in the year 1797:* "De Boigne

* Letter of LONGINUS, to the *Telegraph* newspaper, dated 2nd January, 1797.

" is formed by nature and education to guide and " command: his school acquirements are much above " mediocrity: he is a tolerable Latin scholar, and reads, " writes, and speaks French, Italian, and English, " with ease and fluency. He is not deficient in a " general acquaintance with books, and possesses great " knowledge of the world. He is extremely polite, " affable, pleasant, humorous, and vivacious; elegant in " his manners, resolute in his determinations, and firm " in his measures; remarkably well versed in the " mechanism of the human mind, and has perfect " command over himself. To the political subtlety of " the Italian school he has added consummate Oriental " intrigue; made his approaches to power in disguise, " and only showed himself when too strong to be " resisted. On the grand stage where he has acted a " brilliant and important part for these ten years, he is " dreaded and idolised, feared and admired, respected " and beloved. Latterly the very name of de Boigne " conveyed more terror than the thunder of his " cannons. A singular instance of which I shall relate " *en passant*. Najaf Kúli Khan in his last moments " advised his Begam to resist in the fort of Kanúnd " the efforts of his enemies, who would assuredly grasp, " on his demise, at the small remnants of his patrimony; " 'resist,' said he, 'but if de Boigne appears, yield.' " He will be long regretted, long recollected in India. " His justice was uncommon, and singularly well-" proportioned between severity and relaxation. He

" possessed the happy art of gaining the confidence " of surrounding princes and subjects. He was active " and persevering to a degree which can only be " conceived or believed by those who were spectators of " his indefatigable labours from the time he raised eight " battalions till his departure from his station. I have " seen him daily rise with the sun, survey his *Karkhana* " (arsenal), inspect his troops, enlist recruits, direct the " vast movements of three brigades, raise resources and " encourage manufacturers for their arms, ammunitions, " and stores, harangue in his durbar, give audience to " ambassadors, administer justice, regulate the civil and " revenual affairs of a *Jaidad* (province) of twenty " lakhs of rupees, listen to a multitude of letters from " various parts on various important matters, dictate " replies, carry on an intricate system of intrigue in " different courts, superintend a private trade of a " lakh of rupees, keep his accounts, his private and " public correspondence, and direct and move forward a " most complex political machine. All this he did " without any European assistance. He used to say " that any ambitious person who reposes confidence in " another risks the destruction of his views. * * * * " In person he is above six feet high, giant-boned, large " limbs, strong featured, and with piercing eyes. There " is something in his countenance which depicts the " hero, and compels us to yield implicit obedience. " * * * * * It has often been a subject of sur- " prise to many how de Boigne could so long and so

" invariably aggrandise his power whilst many ad-
" venturers in the same line have repeatedly failed.
" Setting his talents, perseverance, and policy aside,
" there is another cause which is not generally known
" or considered. Other Europeans who have attempted
" the project which de Boigne realised failed from the
" want of a fixed and sufficient fund to pay their troops.
" De Boigne's penetrating genius foresaw and obviated
" this fatal error. Soon after the establishment of his
" two brigades, he persuaded Mádhají Sindia to consign
" some certain pergunnahs for their payments. This
" was done in 1793. A *Jaidad* producing sixteen lakhs
" per annum was granted for the expense of his
" army, which still continues appropriated to that
" purpose. * * * This *Jaidad* has been augmented
" by the attention and equity of de Boigne to twenty
" lakhs a year, and is in as high a state of cultivation
" as the most fertile parts of Banáras; and the ryots
" are as happy as sensual beings can be, abstracted from
" intellectual enjoyments."

This contemporary account is in many points confirmed by the remarks given in the memoir of his life published at Chambéry in 1829. "M. de Boigne," it is there stated, "did not limit his cares to the concerns of his
" army; he directed at the same time his attention to
" the provinces which Sindia had confided to him. He
" introduced into them the greatest order. The
" collection of the public revenue was indeed made by
" the military authorities according to the custom of

" the country. But the amounts to be received had " been settled with justice, and they were fixed. It was " this that caused the collections to be realised with " greater regularity and with less difficulty than is the " case generally in India. He had two offices of " account, the one serving to control the other. In " one, the accounts were kept in French; in the other " all the entries were written in Persian. At the end " of each month the statement of receipts and expendi- " tures was transmitted to the Government.

" It was inevitable that so many details, so multiplied " and so varied, should occupy all the time of the " general; but the importance of his mission, and the " desire by which he was actuated to carry it to a " successful end, inspired him with an activity which " sufficed for everything. He used personally to inspect " the works going on in the arsenal; to visit the parade " ground daily, for some hours, there to make the " troops manœuvre and to pass them in review. From " the parade ground he used to return to his office, " there to attend to administrative matters.

" As the army never ceased to be the particular object " of his attention, his troops became formidable alike " for their numbers and for their perfect discipline. On " this subject we quote the honourable testimony of an " English writer. 'It was not the least of the advan- " ' tages arising from General de Boigne's merit,' writes " the *Bengal Journal* of the 18th September, 1790, " ' that, in his military capacity, he should have "'softened, by means of an admirable perseverance, "'the ferocious and almost savage character of the "'Maráthás. He submitted to the discipline and to "'the civilisation of European armies, soldiers who "'till then had been regarded as barbarians; and to "'such an extent did he succeed, that the rapacious "'licence which had formerly been common amongst "'them came at last to be looked upon as infamous "'even by the meanest soldier.'"

Such was the opinion formed of de Boigne by those who lived in his times and who knew him personally. To us, who can look back on all that he accomplished, and who can form a tolerably accurate idea of the difficulties he must have had to encounter, he stands out as pre-eminently the foremost European figure between the departure of Warren Hastings and the arrival of Marquess Wellesley. It was de Boigne who made it possible for Sindia to rule in Hindostan, at the same time that he controlled the councils of Púna. It was through de Boigne alone that Mádhají's great dream, dissolved by his death, became possible of realisation. But for de Boigne the power of the Maráthás would never have become so formidable, would never have been able to offer a resistance to the British so determined and so prolonged. It was de Boigne who introduced into the North-West Provinces the germs of that civil administration which the English have since successfully developed. I cannot do better, in concluding this sketch of his career, than quote the apposite language of the historian of the fall of the Moghol Empire. "Though moving in an obscure "scene," writes Mr. Keene,* "de Boigne was one of "the great personages of the World's Drama; and "much of the small amount of civil and military "organisation upon which the British Empire of "Hindostan was ultimately founded is due to his "industry, skill, and valour."

* *The Fall of the Moghul Empire*, by Henry George Keene.

II.

The commandants of the several brigades raised by de Boigne and his successors will now come under review. The first brigade, raised in 1792-3, was originally commanded by Colonel Fremont. He was succeeded in 1794 by Colonel Perron; the latter, in 1797, by Colonel Drugeon; he, the following year, by Colonel Duprat; Colonel Duprat, in 1799, by Colonel Sutherland; and Colonel Sutherland, in 1802, by Colonel Pohlmann.

The second brigade was originally commanded by Colonel Perron. On his transfer to the first brigade, in 1794, Major Gardner succeeded him. Major Sutherland replaced Gardner in 1795, and Major Pohlmann Sutherland in 1799. In 1802 Sutherland and Pohlmann changed places, and the following year Sutherland was replaced by Colonel Hessing.

The third brigade was raised in 1795. Its first commandant was Captain Pedrons. He was replaced in 1801 by Major Bourquin.

A fourth brigade was raised in 1803. Of this Colonel Dudrenec was the commandant. A fifth, raised the same year, was allotted to Major Browning.

Besides these there were, in 1803, attached to Sindia's army the following additional brigades: that of Filoze, consisting of eight battalions of infantry, 500 cavalry, and forty-five guns; that of Sombre, composed of six battalions of infantry, 500 cavalry, and thirty-five guns; that of Shepherd, attached to Ambaji Inglia, numbering five battalions, 500 cavalry, and twenty-five guns.

Before proceeding to deal with the men whose names I have mentioned, and some of whom filled a great part in the history of the period, I propose to give a detailed account of the internal economy of the brigades as finally settled by de Boigne.

A brigade was composed of eight battalions. Each battalion comprised within itself infantry and artillery. Each was commanded by a captain, having under him a lieutenant, either European or European by descent. A battalion had eight companies of infantry, each commanded by a subadar, aided by two jemadars, one kót havildar, three havildars, four naicks, and fifty-two sepoys. The artillery of the same battalion consisted of one sergeant-major (European), and five European gunners, one jemadar, one havildar, five naicks, thirty-five gólandáz, five tindals, thirty-five klássis, twenty bildars, thirty gáriwáns, four ironsmiths, and four carpenters. A battalion had also a native surgeon, and a complement of matsadís, water carriers, and the like. Every battalion had 408 stand of arms, four field-pieces, one howitzer, five trumbrils, 120 bullocks, and two native carts. Every gun had constantly ready with it 300 rounds of shot and 100 rounds of grape. A howitzer had fifty stone shells and fifty rounds of grape. The monthly pay of the native officers and men of a battalion was about 4500 rupees. The pay of the officers was as follows:—A colonel received 3000 rupees; a lieutenant-colonel 2000; a major 1200; a captain 400; a captain-lieutenant 300; a lieutenant 200; an ensign 150. These rates were increased fifty per cent. when the officers concerned were serving in the Dekhan. The men received, under the same circumstances, a proportional increase. Besides their pay, officers commanding brigades, whether colonels lieutenant-colonels or majors, received 100 rupees a month as table allowance.

A brigade of eight battalions consisted of 6000 men. Besides the battalion complement of guns above detailed the brigade had attached to it three battering guns and two mortars with men to serve them. Each had likewise 200 irregular cavalry and 500 irregular infantry (Rohillas).

The battalions were named after famous cities or forts, such as Dehli, Agra, Búrhánpúr. The men were disciplined according to the English regulations of 1780, then in force in the British army. The regular infantry were armed with muskets and bayonets manufactured at Agra. The irregulars with match-locks and bayonets. The cavalry were well mounted. Seven hundred of them were armed with match-locks and swords; 500 with carbines, pistols, and swords; they were drilled in the European fashion.*

I propose now to consider the *personnel* of these battalions and brigades. Of the first on the list, Colonel Fremont, I have been unable to collect any interesting details. He would seem to have been amongst the first Frenchmen who joined de Boigne, for I find him commanding a brigade of six battalions in 1792, and storming at their head the hill fort of Báláhárá, sixty miles to the east of Jaipúr. Again, in 1794, he commanded a brigade of eight battalions at an action which took place at Datiá in Bandalkhand. It is probable that he died shortly after that action, for in the year following it, the command of his brigade devolved on Perron, and his name ceases to be mentioned.

Perron was a very remarkable adventurer. He came out to India in the year 1774 as a common sailor on board the French frigate the *Sardaigne*. Being a man of energy, ambition, and strength of will, he quitted the naval service and strove by various means to make a fortune in the country. It was not, however, till he made the acquaintance of de Boigne, in 1789, that he very decidedly ameliorated his condition. De Boigne had just then acceded to the urgent solicitations of

* I have taken all these details from a curious old book, entitled *A Sketch of the rise, progress, and termination of the regular corps formed and commanded by Europeans in the Service of the Native Princes of India*, by Lewis Ferdinand Smith, late Major in Daolát Ráo Sindia's service. The book was published at the beginning of the century, and is very scarce.

Mádhají Sindia by agreeing to re-enter his service. He was in want of officers. Struck by the energetic temper displayed by Perron, he offered him the post of captain-lieutenant in his second brigade. Perron jumped at the offer, and at once distinguished himself and won the heart of his chief by his attention to duty, his courage, and his activity. The camp became his world, and he devoted himself with all the ardour of his nature to take a leading part in it. He distinguished himself so much at the battles of Mirtá and Patan that de Boigne soon after entrusted him with an independent command. He was sent in 1792 with his brigade to reduce the fort of Kanúnd. How he succeeded on this occasion I have related in the preceding section. For this service he was promoted to the rank of major. He then rejoined de Boigne, and was present at the well-contested battle of Lakhairí. The following year he was detached by his chief at the head of his brigade to Púna, to take there also the command of the troops which had accompanied Mádhají Sindia to that court under the command of Hessing and Filoze. His whole regular force amounted then to 18,000 men. He was at Púna when Mádhají died (12th February, 1794).

Into the intrigues which immediately followed the succession of Daolát Ráo Sindia it is not necessary here to enter. It will be sufficient to state that the unsettled condition of affairs at the court of the Péshwa roused the ambition of the Nizám Ali Khan, the Nizám of Haidarabád. This intriguing prince was induced to believe that the power of the Mahommedan rule might be revived in the ruins of Púna. He accordingly assembled an army at Bídr, and advanced thence towards the Maráthá frontier.

Nizám Ali had some reason for his confidence. Besides some 70,000 irregular infantry he had serving in his army 15,000 regulars, commanded by a very famous Frenchman, M. Raymond, a man who had served under Bussy, and whose name still lives revered in the Dekhan. To support these Nizám Ali led into the field 20,000 horsemen and a due proportion of artillery.

To meet this formidable invasion the Péshwa summoned all his vassal chieftains. Daolát Ráo Sindia brought 25,000 men; Rághúji Bhonslá 15,000; Holkar 10,000; Paréshrám Bháo 7000. Other contingents increased the total number to 130,000; and besides these there were 10,000 Pindáris.

But the great strength of the Péshwa's army consisted in the brigades commanded by the *quondam* French sailor. Perron had ten of de Boigne's trained battalions, amounting with cavalry and artillery to about 10,000 men. There were also serving under his orders six battalions commanded by Filoze, amounting with guns and cavalry, to about 5000 men; and four by Hessing, amounting to 3000.

Holkar, too, brought similarly trained troops unto the field, *viz.*, four battalions of about 3000 men, commanded by the Chevalier Dudrenec; and two of 1500 led by Major Boyd.

The two armies met midway between the forts of Kardlá and Parindá. The battle which ensued was the first great departure since the death of Mádhají Sindia from the policy of that great statesman; the first marked deviation from his principle of one general alliance against an enemy who would otherwise destroy them piecemeal. It was fought the 12th March, 1795. The Maráthás occupied a defensive position, of which Perron's troops formed the left. On the high ground near him Perron had placed his artillery, and he supported this arm by the infantry and cavalry in the plain below. The troops of Dudrenec and Boyd were with Holkar in the centre.

The battle began by an advance of the Mahommedans on the right wing and centre of the Maráthás. The attack completely succeeded. The Maráthá right wing was driven on to its centre, at the same time that the centre itself was completely broken by the steady advance of Raymond's drilled troops. These divisions fled in confusion, carrying Dudrenec's and Boyd's men with them, and endeavouring to seek a refuge behind the still unbroken left. Towards this left covered and supported by a cavalry flushed with victory Raymond now advanced. Perron allowed him to approach almost within musket-shot, and then suddenly opened a concentrated and continuous fire from the thirty-five guns loaded with grape which he had placed on the eminence. At the same moment Rághújí Bhonslá assailed the Mahommedan cavalry with a shower of rockets, the materials for firing which he had maintained on the ground during the general fight of the right wing. This simultaneous discharge sent the Moghol cavalry to the right-about. Raymond's infantry, however, not only stood firm, but succeeded for a time in making a successful opposition to all the efforts of Perron. It is difficult to say how the battle would have ended had Nizám Ali been endowed with the most ordinary qualities of a leader. But like most Asiatic commanders he trusted only to his horsemen. When, then, these fled, he fled with them, sending order after order to Raymond to follow him. Meanwhile the Maráthá horse, rallying, were hastening to support Perron. Raymond, then, most unwillingly was forced to follow his master. He did so, however, in the most perfect order, prepared to renew the fight the next day. An accident, however, converted the retreat during the night into a complete rout.* Three days later a humiliating accommodation was forced upon the pusillanimous Nizám.

The battle of Kardlá, if it crushed the Nizám, gave by its results, fuller impetus to the intrigues going on

* This accident is thus related by Grant Duff (Vol. III. chapter VI.). "In the stillness of night a small patrol of Marhátás, in search of water for their horses, come by chance to a rivulet where lay a party of Moghols, who, discovering what they were, instantly fired upon them. Raymond's sentries who were in the neighbourhood, also fired, when their whole line, who lay on their arms, with their muskets loaded as they had retreated, started from their sleep and instantly fired a sort of irregular volley. The alarm which such a discharge of musketry occasioned, in the state of the Moghol army at that moment, may be conceived. * * * Nizám Ali in perfect consternation sought refuge within the walls of Kurdlá.

at Púna, and these received a further accession of force by the untimely death of the youthful Péshwa, Madhú Ráo (October 25th, 1795). An account of these intrigues would be foreign to my present subject. A few months after the Péshwa's death de Boigne resigned to Perron the command of the armies of Sindia in Hindostan.

The fortunate man who had left France as a common sailor now ruled and administered in the name of Sindia the country from Lahore to Kotá and between Aligarh and Jodhpúr. He possessed greater power than any European had till that time possessed in Hindostan. This power he used, according to contemporary authority, in such a manner "as to aggrandise his authority and "his riches."* In his admirable work on the Fall of Moghol Empire, Mr. Keene has extracted from a record published by order of the local Government, a passage bearing upon the mode in which Perron's administration was conducted. "Perron," says this record,† which I extract from Mr. Keene's book, "succeeded in erecting" (a principality) "for the maintenance of the army, and "reigned over it in the plenitude of sovereignty. He "maintained all the state and dignity of an oriental "despot, contracting alliances with the more potent "Rájás, and overawing by his military superiority the "petty chiefs. At Dehli, and within the circle of the "imperial dominions, his authority was paramount to

* Major Ferdinand Smith, before referred to.

† *Aleegurh Statistics.* By J. R. Hutchinson and J. W. Sherer.

" that of the emperor. His attention was chiefly directed " to the prompt realization of revenue. Pargannahs " were generally formed; a few were allotted as *jaidad* " to chiefs on condition of military service; the revenue " (of the lands in the neighbourhood of Aligarh) was " collected by large bodies of troops always concentrated at " head-quarters. A brigade was stationed at Sikandrabád " for the express purpose of realizing collections. In the " event of any resistance on the part of a landholder, who " might be in balance, a severe and immediate example " was made by the plunder and destruction of his " village; and blood was not unfrequently shed in the " harsh and hasty measures which were resorted to. " The arrangements for the administration of justice " were very defective; there was no fixed form of " procedure, and neither Hindú nor Mahommedan law " was regularly administered. The suppression of crime " was regarded as a matter of secondary importance. " There was an officer styled the Bakhshi Adálat whose " business was to receive reports from the Amils (officials) " in the interior, and communicate General Perron's " orders respecting the disposal of any offenders " apprehended by them. No trial was held; the proof " rested on the Amil's report, and the punishment was " left to General Perron's judgment."

The vacillating character of Daolát Ráo Sindia imposed upon Perron difficulties of a character different from those over which de Boigne had triumphed. Daolát Ráo possessed none of the foresight, none of the power of comprehensive view, for which his adoptive father was so famous. The influence wielded by the latter, and inherited for the moment by Daolát Ráo, was frittered away in contests for secondary objects at Púna. Gradually the tried adherents of Mádhají fell away from his successor, and Perron was then called upon to meet as enemies in the field the men who had been the allies and followers of de Boigne.

Foremost amongst these men was Lakhwá Dádá. Lakhwá Dádá was a Maráthá Brahman. He had distinguished himself in the service of Mádhají in 1788 by his brilliant and successful defence of Agra against the Patán leaders. He had fought side by side with de Boigne on many a well-contested field, and especially in the bloody battle of Lakhairí. To none of his adherents had Mádhájí shown greater confidence. Such was the man, clever influential, and far-sighted, whom Daolát Ráo, actuated by the suspicion that he had connived in the escape of the widows of his predecessor from the prison to which he had consigned them, deprived of his power and dismissed from all his employments.

In those days arbitrary power could not always be exercised with impunity towards a clever and influential servant of the State. Lakhwá Dádá knew that a great many powerful vassals were impatient of the yoke of Doalát Ráo; that they wanted only a leader. He threw himself into their ranks, was recognised as their chief, raised a powerful army, repeatedly defeated the troops sent against him, and reduced all the country from

Ujain to Sironj.* Agra, too, the place in which in his younger days he had won his spurs, fell into the hands of his adherents.

Perron had not been blind to the events occurring in his government. In Agra were his arsenals, his magazines, his manufactories. To Agra, then, he marched, at the head of his whole available force. He was joined before the place by Ambají Inglia, one of Daolát Ráo's principal officers, at the head of a large body of cavalry.

Agra resisted long, but Lakhwạ Dádá was not there to defend it in person, and in the end it surrendered. Perron then marched against Lakhwá Dádá, who had by this time mastered nearly two-thirds of Rájputáná. The hostile forces met at Sondia, in the Datiá territory, on the 3rd May 1800. The disciplined battalions prevailed. Lakhwá Dádá was beaten and so severely wounded that he died shortly after.

Rid of this formidable adversary Perron had time to turn his attention to George Thomas, an adventurer who had almost succeeded, single handed, in firmly establishing an independent principality in northern India. Thomas was a very remarkable man. An Irishman by birth, Thomas had come out to India as a common sailor on board of an English man-of-war about the year 1782. Deserting from his ship as she lay anchored in the Madras roads, he had wandered about the Carnatic, and had finally taken service under the

* Grant Duff.

Bígam Sombre. A bold, indefatigable, active man, endowed with great natural abilities and a large share of common-sense, possessing, too, a handsome person and a winning manner, Thomas was just the man to rise to distinction under such a mistress. Opportunities did not fail him. In April, 1788, when the contingent of the Bígam was serving under the orders of the Emperor Shah Alim at the siege of Gókalgarh, Thomas was fortunate enough to save the Emperor from death or a worse captivity. For five years Thomas continued in the service of the Bígam, and it is probable that, as time went on, he began to aspire to a position of a more intimate character. But, if he did entertain such a hope, he was disappointed. A Frenchman named Le Vaisseau supplanted him. Thomas upon this left the Bígam's service and set up for himself. He went first to the village of Anúpshahr where was stationed the frontier brigade of the English force. From this place he corresponded with Appú Khandí Ráo, an influential officer in the service of Sindia. The correspondence ended by Thomas obtaining from his friend the investiture of a few villages at Maráthá territory. Subsequently Thomas obtained permission to conquer and administer the district of Hariáná, a part of the country so neglected and desolate that up to that time no one had considered it worth taking. He first succeeded in taking a large village in Hariáná. His subsequent proceedings are thus described by a personal friend and contemporary: *

* Major Ferdinand Smith.

"Thomas commenced his ambitious career in 1794, "after he left the Bígam Sombre's service, by collecting "a few men near Dehli, with whom he stormed a large "village. The little money he acquired from this "village laid the foundation for his future hopes and "prospects; he made a few guns, enlisted more men, "raised two battalions, and besieged parts of the "desolated country of Hariáná. * * * He increased "his forces by plunder; the brass and copper vessels "he found in the towns and villages were melted into "cannon, and cannon procured him money. Thus he "proceeded some time, gradually raising his forces as "he augmented his means to pay them, until 1797, "when they amounted to four battalions. He then "cleared away the jungle from the abandoned fort of "Hánsí, and put it in a state of defence. His range "of depredations now became more extensive and his "resources greater. At last, in 1801, he raised his "party to ten battalions with sixty pieces of cannon, "and secured a country to himself of three lakhs a "year."

Such, in brief, is the outline of the history of the rise of George Thomas. But there are other details, not uninteresting, which served to help him on. Such was his adoption by Appú Khandi Ráo immediately subsequent to their joint visit to Dehli in 1794 to receive investiture of their fiefs from the local representative of Daolát Ráo Sindia. It was on this occasion that Appú Khándí conferred upon Thomas the right to occupy Hariáná, and extended the powers he had previously granted to him. Another characteristic incident of this part of his career was the restoration by his means of his old mistress, the Bígam Sombre, now once more a widow, to the principality of which she had been deprived by the intrigues of her officers. A third, the invariable fidelity and forbearance he displayed towards his adoptive father, notwithstanding the repeated intrigues, amounting often to treachery, indulged in by the latter. Latterly he recognised Ambají Inglia, the favourite general of Sindia, as his most trusted ally.

Before proceeding to the event which brought Thomas into collision with Perron, I propose to devote a few lines to the manner of his administration of Hánsi and its surrounding district. The story is best told in his own words.* "Here," writes he in his memoirs, "I "established my capital, re-built the walls of the city, "which had long since fallen to decay, and repaired the "fortifications. As it had been long deserted, at first "I found difficulty in procuring inhabitants, but by "degrees, and gentle treatment, I selected between "5000 and 6000 persons, to whom I allowed every "lawful indulgence. I established a mint, and coined "my own rupees, which I made current in my army "and country; cast my own artillery, commenced "making muskets, match-locks, and powder; * * * "till at length," he goes on to say, "having gained

* Francklin's *Life of George Thomas.*

"a capital and country bordering on the Sikh territories, "I wished to put myself in a capacity, when a "favourable opportunity should offer, of attempting "the conquest of the Panjáb, and aspired to the honour "of placing the British standard on the banks of the "Attock." No ignoble aspiration, indeed, for a deserter from a British man-of-war!

It was no idle dream however. Thomas had, in fact, already left his own territory to make the attempt, and he was actually within four marches of Láhor, when he received an express to the effect that his principality of Hariáná was menaced by Perron.

The fact is that Perron, wielding the power of Sindia in Hindostan, having crushed Lakhwá Dádá, was not disposed to brook the establishment so near to Dehli of an independent power, and that power wielded by a native of Great Britain. He accordingly sent to Thomas a summons to repair to Dehli, there to do homage as a vassal of Sindia. Anticipating his refusal he massed ten battalions and 2000 horses at Dehli. Thomas, foreseeing what was in store for him, sent an indignant reply, at the same time that he made every effort to return and cover his capital. Marching thirty or forty miles a day he succeeded in reaching Hánsi before Perron had moved out of Dehli.

But Perron had committed himself too far to retreat. He had allied himself with the Sikhs and obtained from them assistance alike in men and money. Thomas likewise had formed alliances with his old friend the

Bígam Sombre, with the Rájás of Jaipúr and Alwar, and with Lafontaine, who commanded six battalions of Filoze's brigade in the service of Sindia. Reinforced by the troops received from these quarters he met Perron's army at Báhádúrgarh, eighteen miles to the west of Dehli. Neither party was very confident of success. Perron thought, moreover, that it might be possible to arrange matters satisfactorily without having recourse to the doubtful arbitrament of a battle. He therefore commissioned one of his officers, Major Lewis Ferdinand Smith,* to repair to the camp of Thomas, and to offer him 60,000 rupees a month for his troops, the rank of colonel for himself, and the fort of Hánsi in perpetuity, provided he would take service under Sindia, and acknowledge Perron as his chief. Thomas, though unwillingly, consented to discuss these terms at a personal interview.

There were many reasons which combined to dissuade Thomas from the offered accommodation. Intelligence had but just reached him of the defeat of Daolát Ráo's troops at Ujjén, and of his precipitate retreat on Búrhánpúr. Letters too had come in from Jeswant Ráo Holkar urging him to attack Perron, and promising him aid in men and money. Recruits, too, were on their way to join him, whilst he knew that Sindia was demanding reinforcements from Perron. His policy was plainly to temporise until he should possess a

* It is from the memoirs of this officer, an actor on the scene, that I have gleaned the details which follow.

manifest superiority. This indeed, was the course that recommended itself to his clearer vision. But the demand made by Perron at the interview, that he should divide his force and send one-half to the assistance of Sindia maddened him to such an extent that he broke off the conference and hastily retreated to Hánsi.

On the breaking up of the conference Perron returned immediately to Aligarh, called thither by the necessity of attending to the urgent requisitions of Sindia, leaving his force before Báhádúrgarh under the command of Major Bourquin, then acting as commandant of the third brigade. This officer at once despatched Major Smith to besiege Georgegarh, a fort which had been built by Thomas, about seventy miles from Hánsi, whilst he himself should cover the siege. Thomas, however, noticing the distance of the covering from the besieging force, broke up suddenly from Hánsi, fell upon Smith and completely defeated him. What he might have accomplished may be gathered from Major Smith's own words: "I was attacked," he writes,* "by Thomas "with eight battalions, compelled to raise the siege and "retreat to Jajar, four *coss* (eight miles) to the east of "Georgegarh; favoured by the obscurity of the night, "I was not completely cut off, and made good my "retreat, with the loss of one gun and one-third of my "force killed and wounded. How I escaped total "destruction I do not yet know. Why Thomas did not

* *Sketch of the rise and progress of regular corps under Sindia*, by Major L. F. Smith.

" follow my retreat I cannot say, for if he had continued " the pursuit I must have lost all my guns, and my " party would have been completely destroyed."

After raising the siege Thomas threw himself into Georgegarh, the defences of which he strengthened. Here he was attacked on the 20th September by Bourquin's troops, who had marched seventy miles in the thirty-six hours almost immediately preceding the assault. "Bourquin," writes Major Smith, "did not " lead the attack himself, but prudently remained with " the cavalry, 2000 yards in rear of George Thomas's " line. The seven battalions of de Boigne, with calm " intrepidity advanced with their guns through heavy " sand, exposed to a dreadful and well-directed fire of " fifty-four pieces of cannon, and attacked Thomas's " ten battalions in their intrenchments; but they were " repulsed with the severe loss of 1100 men killed and " wounded, which was nearly one-third of their number. " * * Thomas's loss was not so great, as the guns " of de Boigne's battalions were mostly dismounted by " their recoil on the sand, when fired, which snapt their " axle-trees."

"Had Thomas," adds Major Smith, "taken advantage " of Bourquin's ignorance and folly, and sallied out on " the beaten troops of Perron, he would have overturned " his power, but Thomas at this critical moment was " confused and confounded." Thomas indeed, took no advantage of their repulse. He remained shut up in Georgegarh waiting for the reinforcements promised by Holkar, and which never came; for before the period then passing, the power of Holkar, though he knew it not, had been temporarily annihilated at Indúr.

Meanwhile reinforcements poured into the besieger's camp. The incapable Bourquin was superseded by Colonel Pedrons, and he turned the siege into a blockade. This lasted for seven weeks. Reduced then by famine and desertion, having spent his ammunition and finding his remaining troops utterly disorganised, Thomas saw that the end was at hand. Rather, however, than surrender he mounted—the night of the 10th November 1801—his Persian horse, and accompanied by his only two European officers, Captain Hearsey and Lieutenant Birch, and some troops, rode away, hoping to reach Hánsi by a circuitous route. The party, though attacked and pursued, arrived safely at Hánsi on the third day.

Colonel Pedrons consigned to Bourquin the task of finishing the war. The latter followed up Thomas to Hánsi, laid siege to the place, and though Thomas defended himself stoutly, there could be no doubt of the ultimate issue. An offer made by a portion of the garrison to betray their leader brought matters to a crisis. Major Smith was again detached to communicate with Thomas, to inform him of the treachery of his troops, and to offer him honourable terms. These terms assured him freedom of action for himself within British territory with the safe conduct of the property still remaining to him. Thomas accepted the conditions

(1st January 1802), and proceeded towards Calcutta with the intention of returning to his native land with the wreck of his fortune amounting then, according to Major Smith, to a lakh of rupees. He died, however, on his way down, near Barhámpúr, in the burying-ground of which place he was interred. His career, records the friend already quoted "was more worthy of "astonishment than imitation."

Perron was now complete master of the situation. He had beaten all his master's enemies in Hindostan; his master's troops had triumphed in Ujjén. But his double triumph had similarly affected both master and servant. They showed, in this crisis of their fortunes, that prosperity was fatal to them. It exhalted their pride and weakened their judgment.

Perron had had no education, no mental training; he was not gifted with a large mind. A self-made man, he had raised himself from the position of a common sailor to a post which was, in fact, second only to one other in India, and, so long as he had enemies to fight, the animal vigour of his nature had a fit field for its display. But with the dispersion of his enemies the scene of action for that animal vigour disappeared, and his mental power was more largely called upon. In this respect Perron was weak. He began to show undue contempt for the native chieftains; an unjust partiality for his own countrymen; to further his own private interest only; to look upon the interests of Sindia as secondary, not to be placed in the balance against his own.

It was not long before the action based upon such views raised a storm against him. One after another the native chiefs and leaders complained to Sindia of the arrogance and grasping character of his French lieutenant. To meet the storm raised by these denunciations, Perron proceeded at the end of 1802 to the court of Daolát Ráo then held at Ujjén. He proposed to himself three objects in this visit. The first, to ascertain the views of Colonel Collins, the British resident, then at Sindia's court; the second, to ascertain by personal examination how far Colonel Sutherland, who commanded the second brigade, and whose character he dreaded, was likely to supplant him; the third, to destroy the effect of the intrigues of Sákharám Ghatgay, Sindia's father-in-law, and of the other chiefs who were hostile to him. Should he find the position too strong for him he had resolved to resign his office.

Perron did not resign. He presented to Daolát Ráo a *nazzar* of five lakhs of rupees, and seemed to triumph. After a stay of a few weeks only at Ujjén he returned to Aligarh with his former power confirmed. An incident occurred shortly afterwards, however, which roused all his fears and suspicions.

The student of Indian history of that period will recollect that the defeat of Sindia's army by Jeswant Ráo Holkar near Púna on the 25th October, 1802, had caused the Péshwa to fly in trepidation from his capital. From Severndrúg, where he had taken refuge, the Péshwa addressed pressing solicitations to Sindia, still in camp at Ujjén, to come to his aid. It may freely be asserted that the fate of India was in the hands of Daolát Ráo. Had he marched to the aid of his suzerain, not only would no treaty of Bassein have been signed, but he would have attained, with one bound, the influence and power of his predecessor.

Daolát Ráo cast away the opportunity—never to recur. Why did he do so? Was it, as he gave out, that he was not strong enough, or did he doubt the intention of the Péshwa to throw himself, unless relieved, in the hands of the British?

A glance at the relations between Daolát Ráo and M. Perron at this period will tend to elucidate the question. Perron had hardly returned to Aligarh before he received from Daolát Ráo a pressing requisition to send him another brigade, as with his then force he was not strong enough to march to the assistance of the Péshwa. Daolát Ráo had then three brigades with him; one, belonging to Perron's force, commanded by Sutherland; one, an independent brigade, commanded by Filoze; and a third belonging to the Bígam Sombre. Perron had with himself three brigades. When, therefore, he received the requisition to send one of these to Ujjén, he thought he read in the order a resolution to despoil him of his power. Although, then, he saw that the moment was critical, that by delaying to comply he risked the independence and even the existence of the Maráthá empire, yet regard for his own interests and the dread of throwing too much power into the hands of

Daolát Ráo, caused him to hesitate for three months. When at last he did comply, the favourable moment had passed, and the Péshwa had thrown himself into the arms of the British Government for protection. In February, 1803, Perron despatched to Ujjén the fourth brigade under Dudrenec, and half of the newly-raised fifth brigade under Brownrigg. But it was too late. The treaty of Bassein had been signed.

The treaty of Bassein precipitated the conflict between Sindia and the British. It roused Daolát Ráo to a sense of his errors. In that treaty he saw not only the subversion of the vast plans of his predecessor but a threat against himself. Though invited to become a party to the defensive portion of the treaty he distinctly refused. Then probably for the first time in his life he understood the conception of Mádhají, finding himself as he did face to face with the dangers which Mádhají's scheme would have rendered impossible. Then he bestirred himself; then, at last, he sought to unite the Maráthás against the common foe. But he was too late. Holkar refused to join him. His preparations, though he sought to conceal and did deny them, were too patent. The Governor-General of India, Marquess Wellesley, resolved then to anticipate him, and to bring the matter to the arbitrament of the sword. War was declared, and on the 8th August, 1803, an English force under General Lake crossed the frontier of Sindia's territory and marched straight on Aligarh.

Perron was at Aligarh, but he was as a general without an army. The main body of the troops were with Daolát Ráo; others were not at the moment amenable to his orders. He had with him at the time but 2000 infantry and 8000 cavalry.

But there were other evils threatening him which Perron dreaded far more than a deficiency of troops. His conduct in the early part of the year, which I have detailed at length, had roused all the suspicions of Daolát Ráo. His disgrace, again imminent, was hastened by the present of fifteen lakhs of rupees made by Ambají Inglia to Daolát Ráo as the price of the Subadárship of Hindostan. Ambají was one of the great chiefs whom Perron had insulted, and from whom he could expect no mercy. His rival would have drained his purse if not his life's blood.

Perron could not even trust the commanders of his brigades. Dudrenec, on his way back from Ujjén to Aligarh, was far more attached to Ambají than to him; Bourquin, who at the moment had the second and third brigades under his orders, threw off his allegiance. But one chance remained, and that was to make the best possible terms with the British.

To this course Perron resigned himself. When, on the 29th August, 1803, General Lake marched on the the village of Aligarh, a splendid opportunity offered to Perron to charge it with the 8000 horse he had under his command. He did not seize it. He gave no orders. His men were paralysed by his indecision, and a few rounds from the galloper guns sent them flying in all directions. Perron fled with them, directing his course first to Hatrás, thence to Mathurá. From this latter place he sent, on the 5th September, a proposal to the English general to surrender on receiving an assurance of protection for his person and his property.

Lord Lake acceded to the proposal. Whereupon, Perron, having first sent his family to Agra, slipped quietly across the river, and, making his way to Sasní, threw himself under the protection of the British detachment stationed there. Thence he was allowed to proceed with his family and his property to Chándarnagar. From that time he and his affairs ceased to interest the Indian world.

III.

Amongst the French officers mentioned in the section is Colonel Pedrons. He must have joined de Boigne early, as he raised and commanded the third brigade in 1795. The next mention I find of him is of so late a date as 1800. In that year, when Perron was engaged in besieging the fort of Agra, Pedrons, then a major, was despatched with eight battalions to attack and annihilate Lakhwá Dádá in Bandalkhand. In this enterprise he was assisted by Ambají Inglia with some irregular infantry and 5000 horse. He found, however, Lakhwá Dádá so strongly posted, that though the latter had only 6000 horse, 3000 Rohillas, and 200 drilled sepoys* under his command, Pedrons was afraid to attack him. He spent two months in fruitless reconnoitering. At the end of that time Perron himself came down and crushed Lakhwá Dádá with one blow (3rd May, 1800). We next hear of Pedrons as relieving

* The 200 sepoys were drilled and commanded by Major Tone, "an unfortunate gentleman," says Major Smith, "whose abilities and integrity were as great as his misfortunes were severe." Major Tone was subsequently shot through the head, whilst serving under Holkar, at an action near Cholí Máhásúr, in 1802. He wrote a valuable work called "Letters on the Maráthá People." (Ferdinand Smith.)

Bourquin in the campaign against Thomas. The part he then took has been already related. His final act was the defence of the fort of Aligarh against an English army under Lord Lake.

I have already stated that when the English army marched on Aligarh Perron had with him only 2000 infantry and 8000 cavalry. The infantry he threw into the fort, the command of which was confided to Pedrons.

Lord Lake's first act was to summon Pedrons to surrender. Pedrons in becoming terms refused. Lord Lake, then, finding that to attack it in the regular form would give the enemy time to concentrate their forces to oppose him, resolved to attempt a *coup de main*.

It was a daring experiment, for Aligarh was strong, well garrisoned, and the country round it had been levelled. It had but one weak point, and that was a narrow passage across the ditch into the fort. This passage was, however, guarded by a strong gateway, and three other gateways had to be forced before the body of the place could be entered. To resolve to attempt such a place by a *coup de main* required no ordinary nerve. The whole future of the campaign depended on the success of the storm. Should it fail, all India would rise up against the English; should it succeed, the Maráthá Empire would receive its death-blow.

But throughout his career Lord Lake always acted on the principle, so often referred to in this work, that "boldness is prudence." He stormed and carried

Aligarh. By that success he paralysed the Maráthá confederacy. To use the words of a contemporary writer then in the service of Sindia, "it was a mortal "blow to the Maráthá war: it struck a panic into the "minds of the natives and astonished all the princes of "Hindostan: it gave them dreadful ideas of European "soldiers and European courage."

Pedrons was taken prisoner at Aligarh. From that time he disappeared from the scene.

The next in order is the Bourquin referred to in the preceding section. This man's real name was Louis Bernard. His previous history and his reason for changing his name are alike unknown to me. It is only known that Perron had raised him from obscurity to the command of a brigade. His campaign against Thomas has been already related. He is next heard of as evincing his gratitude to Perron by revolting against him on the eve of the war with the English. By Perron's flight to British territory and by Pedrons's captivity, Bourquin became the senior officer in command of the old brigades of de Boigne.

Bourquin was close to Dehli, at the head of the second and third brigades, when the English were marching on Aligarh. Another French officer, Colonel Drugeon, was commanding the fort of Dehli. Bourquin, strongly sensible of the political advantage which might arise from having in his camp the blind old Emperor, called upon Drugeon to send him out under an escort. Drugeon refused. Upon this Bourquin prepared to besiege Dehli, and he only desisted when the fatal intelligence of the storming of Aligarh recalled him to a sense of his position.

On receiving this news Bourquin began to cross the Jamná with his two brigades. He had already (11th September) passed over twelve battalions, with seventy pieces of cannon, and 5000 cavalry, when, at eleven o'clock, the English army appeared in sight. Bourquin drew up his troops in a remarkably strong position, his front covered by a line of intrenchments prepared on the two preceding days; each flank covered by a swamp, and his guns hidden by long grass. Wishing to entice the English to attack this formidable position, he directed the outposts to fire on the English camp. At the time that this firing commenced the British troops had grounded their arms, many were undressed, others had gone in search of fuel. Lord Lake, however, hastily collected his men and led them to the attack. The fire from the long grass was, however, so heavy, and the intrenchments were so formidable, that Lord Lake, after losing many men and being wounded himself, stopped the advance to attempt a *ruse de guerre*. He then ordered his cavalry, which was leading, to retire slowly behind the infantry. The movement of the cavalry to the rear induced, in the mind of the French leader, the supposition that the British force was beaten. He ordered the men to leave the intrenchments and complete the victory. This they did with loud shouts. Their error continued till the sudden disappearance of the cavalry showed them the British infantry advancing to meet them. The disciplined battalions fought well, but they were overmatched. Bourquin was the first to leave the field. The rout was then complete. Bourquin surrendered, with five officers, three days later, to the English, and disappeared not only from the field of battle, but from the field of history.

A character superior in every way to Bourquin was the Chevalier Dudrenec. A native of Brest, the son of a commodore in the French navy, Dudrenec had come out to India as a midshipman in a French man-of-war about the year 1774. Why he left the French navy, or the occupation to which he betook himself after leaving it, I have never been able to ascertain. He first appears upon the Indian scene in command of Bígam Sombre's brigade. He left this command in 1791 to join Túkají Holkar, by whom he was commissioned to raise, drill, and equip four battalions on the principle previously employed for Sindia by de Boigne. Dudrenec acquitted himself of this commission with great success. The following year, however, his battalions were destroyed—the men dying at their posts—at the fatal battle of Lakhairí, an account of which I have given in the sketch of de Boigne's career. Not disheartened, Holkar commissioned Dudrenec to raise four more battalions. This task he successfully accomplished, and with them, on the 12th March, 1795, he contributed to the victory of Kardlá, gained by the combined Maráthá forces against the Nizám.

For some time after this engagement Dudrenec remained in comparative inaction at Indúr. In 1797 he added two battalions to his force. In the struggle for power which followed the death of Túkají the same year (1797), Dudrenec sided at first with the legitimate, but imbecile, heir, Khási Ráo. Acting in his name, he alternately defeated, and was defeated by, the pretender, Jeswant Ráo. When at length the triumph of the latter seemed assured, Dudrenec went over with all his troops and guns to his side. But Jeswant Ráo did not trust him, and Dudrenec soon saw that his disgrace was determined upon. Under these circumstances he thought he would try and steal a march upon his master. Taking advantage of the hostilities then engaged between Sindia and Jeswant Ráo (1801) he endeavoured to take his six battalions bodily over to the former. But the men were more faithful than their commander. They drove Dudrenec from the camp and marched to Jeswant Ráo, who at once placed at their head an Englishman named Vickers.

Dudrenec was, however, well received by Sindia, and entrusted with the command of a brigade—the fourth—and placed under the orders of Perron, at Aligarh. In February, 1803, he was detached with this brigade to join Sindia at Ujjén; again, towards the autumn of the same year, when hostilities with the English were imminent, he was sent back to rejoin Perron. This force reached the vicinity of Agra in October, having been joined in its way by the three battalions of

Bourquin's force which had not crossed the Jamná, nor been engaged in the battle of Dehli against the English, and by some other fugitives. The whole force amounted to about 12,000 men, well supplied with excellent artillery.

It was this army, indeed, which fought the famous battle of Láswári. But when it fought that battle Dudrenec was not with it. Influenced, it seems probable, by the example of his fellow adventurers, and by the favourable conditions offered,* he had surrendered (30th October) to the English. His Indian career then closed.

One of the oldest officers in the service of de Boigne was John Hessing, a man who, if not a Dutchman,† was at least of Dutch extraction. He joined de Boigne shortly after the latter entered the service of Sindia, and was present at the hardly-contested battles of Lálsót, of Agra, and of Chaksána. At Patan too, he fought bravely and well. After that battle, however, he quarrelled with de Boigne and tendered his resignation. This was accepted. Sindia then advanced him money to raise a battalion which should be peculiarly his own, and should act as his special body-guard. As com-

* These conditions generally were security of life and property, and permission to return to Europe.

† Grant Duff says he was an Englishman; but his acquaintance and contemporary, Lewis Ferdinand Smith, invariably speaks of him as a foreigner. His name does not appear in the list of British subjects serving Maráthá States, who were pensioned by the British Government, and the inscription on his tomb at Agra declares him a Dutchman.

mandant of this body-guard Hessing accompanied Mádhají to Púna in 1792, augmenting it gradually, as he proceeded, to four battalions. It was at this strength when failing health forced Hessing to leave Púna. He was sent thence to command at Agra where he died in 1803.

His son, George Hessing, succeeded him at Púna. Shortly after that Mádhají Sindia died. Daolát Ráo, however, not only continued his favour to Hessing, but authorised him to increase the number of his battalions to eight. They were at this strength when hostilities broke out between Holkar and Sindia in 1801, although half the number only were then with Daolát Ráo in his camp at Búrhánpúr, George Hessing having sent four to reinforce his father at Agra.

Holkar having shown a disposition at this period to attack and plunder Ujjén, Sindia detached George Hessing, with three of his battalions and one belonging to Filoze, to defend that place. Shortly after he had left, Sindia, not thinking his force strong enough, sent his fourth battalion, and another of Filoze's, under Captain McIntyre, to reinforce him. These were followed by Sindia's grand park of fifty-two guns, the advanced guard of which was formed by two of Perron's battalions under Captain Gautier, and the rear guard by two more under Captain Brownrigg.

Never, in his brilliant career, did Jeswant Ráo Holkar display to a greater extent the qualities of a general than on this occasion. Noticing the distance that separated these parties the one from the other; that the state of the soil, knee-deep with the mud created by the heavy rainfall, precluded the possibility of quick communication between them, at the same time that it rendered the progress of the guns extremely slow, he passed the leading column (George Hessing's) close to Ujjén, and dashed down upon McIntyre's two battalions at Núrí, thirty-five miles from that place. His force was so overwhelming that, notwithstanding their obstinate resistance, he, in the end, forced them to surrender. Having thus placed an impassable distance between Hessing's detachment and the troops under Gautier and Brownrigg, he turned back and fell upon the former. The battle was long, obstinate, and bloody. The immensely superior fire of Holkar's artillery alone decided the day, nor was it until seven* out of his enemy's eleven European officers had been killed, and three taken prisoners; until three-fifths likewise of their men had been killed and one-fifth wounded, that victory decided in favour of Holkar.

George Hessing is next heard of at Agra, commanding at that place when it was threatened by Lord Lake in

* Lewis Ferdinand Smith writes:—"Of the eleven European officers who were in this severe action eight were British subjects, seven of whom were killed at their posts, and only one survived, but survived with wounds. Colonel Hessing, the commander, escaped." The names of the eight British subjects were Graham, Urquhart, Montague, Macpherson, Lang, Doolun, Haden, and Humpherstone. The seven first-named were killed, the last-named was severely wounded and taken prisoner. The names of the foreign officers were Hessing, Dupont, and Derridon. The first escaped, the two last were taken prisoners.

October, 1803. The troops, however, noticing the facility with which their foreign officers had surrendered to the English, placed Hessing and the six officers with him under restraint. This action on their part did not prevent Lord Lake from taking Agra. All the European officers, foreign and English, then within its walls renounced the service of Sindia, and accepted the liberal conditions offered by Marquess Wellesley. Among these was George Hessing.

Michel Filoze, a Neapolitan of low birth and of no education, had at first served under de Boigne. By means of intrigue, however, he contrived to obtain authority to raise a battalion under his own sole command, and at the head of this he accompanied Mádhají to Púna in 1792.

This battalion became the nucleus of the brigade of fourteen battalions raised by Michel Filoze and his son and successor, Fidele, between that year and 1800. At the head of six of these he rendered good service at the battle of Kardlá, 1795. Michel Filoze was an adventurer of the lowest type. To other bad qualities he added the practise of treachery and dishonour. During the intrigues at Púna which followed the death of Mádhají Filoze ingratiated himself with Náná Farnawis, the minister of the Péshwa. When the latter was pressed by Sindia to visit him, and only hesitated because he mistrusted the intentions of Daolát Ráo, Michel Filoze assured him in the most solemn manner, and on his word of honour, that he would guarantee his safe and immediate return to his house. Yet, notwithstanding his oaths, and the pledge of his honour, Filoze himself arrested the Náná on his return from the interview (31st December, 1797) and made him over to his master. This act of his was resented in the most marked manner by the other adventurers at the court and in the camp of Daolát Ráo. They considered this baseness on the part of one of their number as a stain upon themselves as a body. When shortly afterwards, the Náná was released and restored to power, Michel Filoze, dreading his vengeance, fled to Bombay.

He was succeeded by his son Fidele. Fidele Filoze accompanied Daolát Ráo in his campaign against Holkar in 1801 at the head of six battalions. One of these, under Captain McIntyre, was cut off by Jeswant Ráo Holkar at Núrí; a second under George Hessing was destroyed at Ujjén (June 1801); the remaining four took part in the battle of Indúr (14th October, 1801). On this occasion Sindia's army, really commanded by an Englishman, Major Sutherland, gained a decisive victory. Strange to say, after that battle, to the gain of which he and his troops contributed, Fidele Filoze cut his throat. "The reasons for this suicide," writes Major L. F. Smith, so often referred to, "are various. Some "say that he had carried on a traitorous correspondence "with Jeswant Ráo Holkar previous to the battle of "Indúr, and that he cut his throat to prevent the "disgrace of condign punishment; others that he "committed the act in a delirium." Major Smith describes Fidele Filoze as having been "a good, ignorant " man, a much better character than his faithless and " treacherous father, who had all the bad qualities of a " low Italian, and none of the good points which " Italians possess." The Filoze family ultimately settled at Gwáliár.

A great deal might be written regarding the careers of adventurers who were not foreigners but Englishmen, and some of whom displayed the highest qualities. Prominent amongst these stand the names of Sutherland, Smith, Shepherd, Gardner, Skinner, Bellasis, Dodd, Brownrigg, Vickers and Ryan. The first five of these accepted the terms offered by Marquess Wellesley in 1803, and with upwards of thirty other officers renounced the service of native chiefs; the last five were murdered or killed in action.

Of other Frenchmen who did good service to Sindia and Holkar, may be mentioned Captain Plumet, of whom Major Smith records that he was a "Frenchman " and a gentleman, two qualities which were seldom " united in the Maráthá army. He was a man of " respectable character and sound principles." Plumet commanded four battalions for Holkar in the attack on George Hessing at Ujjén (June 1801), and he shared in the defeat inflicted upon Holkar by Major Brownrigg at Barkésar in the July following. Finding Jeswant Ráo Holkar a master difficult to serve, cunning, capricious, and ungrateful, Plumet left him, and returned to the Isle of France.

With these names I have exhausted the list of the principal foreign adventurers who built up the armies of Holkar and Sindia between 1787 and 1803. It is true that many more names remain on the list, but not one that calls for sympathy or interest. This is my own conviction formed upon a minute examination of every paper of that period upon which I have been able to lay my hand. How far that conviction is borne out by contemporary opinion may be gathered from the following sentence culled from Major Smith's work already quoted. "Perron's army," wrote that gentleman in 1805, "was a minute miniature of the French "revolution. Wretches were raised from cooks, bakers, "and barbers, to majors and colonels, absurdly entrusted with the command of brigades, and shoved "into paths to acquire lakhs. This was the quintessence "of *égalité*, and the *acmé* of the French revolution." Even if Major Smith's description be exaggerated, this at least is certain, that of all the men to whom I have referred, but one only, de Boigne, was worthy of representing France. He was worthy; and there was another, Raymond, whose deeds have yet to be recorded, who at least rivals him in the esteem which living, he earned; which, dead, is still not denied him.

IV.

Before proceeding to Raymond it seems fit that I should briefly notice the career of two adventurers, very famous in their day, who flourished at a period immediately antecedent to that of de Boigne. I allude to Madoc and Sombre.

The real name of Sombre, as he was styled on account of his dark complexion, was Walter Reinhard. By birth he was a German, by trade a butcher. He originally came out to India in the Swiss company of infantry under the command of Captain Zeigler, attached to the Bombay European regiment. With that company he most probably came round to the coast, where he deserted and made his way round to Bengal, apparently in the French service.*

After the capture of Chándarnagar in 1757 Sombre wandered from the court of one petty chieftain to that of another in quest of service. After several unimportant adventures he was in 1762 appointed to the command of a brigade of troops in the service of Mír Kásim, Nawáb Názim of Bengal.

Shortly after that event the greed and avidity of the

* Broome's *History of the Bengal Army.*

English rulers of Bengal* forced Mír Kásim to war. The contest was on the one side for dominion, on the other for independence. On the 1st July, 1763, Mr. Ellis and the English garrison of Patna, who had taken and then abandoned that city, surrendered to Mír Kásim's generals, Markar and Sombre, and were sent back thither as prisoners. On the 17th July following, Mír Kásim's main army was repulsed on the banks of the river Adjí by a strong artillery force under Lieutenant Glenn; and two days later it was defeated by Major Adams in the most obstinately contested battle of Katwá.

The brigade of Sombre was not engaged on these occasions, but it joined the main army in time to take party in the bloody battle of Ghériá (2nd August). In this battle Sombre occupied a very prominent position, and had he displayed the smallest pluck, the British power might have been temporarily extinguished on that well-contested field. The left wing of the English had been broken; their centre had been attacked in the rear. The brigades of Sombre and Markar† had only to advance and the day was gained. But it was against Sombre's principle to advance. His plan of action was invariably to draw his men in a line, fire a few shots, form a square, and retreat. He followed out this plan to the letter at Ghériá. He allowed the victory to slip from his grasp, but he covered the retreat of the army.

* Broome's *History of the Bengal Army.*

† Markar was an Armenian in Mír Kásím's service.

The victory of Ghériá was followed up by another (5th September) on the U'dwá nullah; and on the 1st October by the capture of Manghír. In the first defeat Sombre and his brigade were sharers.

The fall of Manghír irritated Mír Kásim to such a degree that he determined to take the terrible revenge of slaughtering the English prisoners held by him at Patna. The story is thus told in his admirable history by the late Colonel Broome.* "Mír Kásim now issued "the fatal order for the massacre of his unfortunate "prisoners, but so strong was the feeling on the subject, "that none amongst his officers could be found to "undertake the office, until Sombre offered his services "to execute it.

"The majority of the prisoners were confined in a "house belonging to one Hadjí Ahmad, on the site of "the present English cemetery in that city. Hither "Sombre repaired on the 5th October, with two "companies of his sipáhis, having on the previous day, "under pretence of giving the party an entertainment "procured all their knives and forks, so that they were "deprived of every means of resistance. Having "surrounded the house, he sent for Messrs. Ellis, Hay, "and Lushington, who went out with six other "gentlemen, and were immediately cut to pieces in the "most barbarous manner and their remains thrown "into a well. The sipáhis now mounted the roof of

* Broome's *History of the Bengal Army*, a standard work based entirely on authentic records.

" the house, which was built in the form of a square, " and fired down upon the remainder of the party, who " were congregated in the centre court. Those who " escaped this volley sought shelter in the building, but " were quickly followed by Sombre's sipáhis, and a " fearful scene of slaughter ensued. The English, " driven to desperation, defended themselves with " bottles, bricks, and articles of furniture; and their " very executioners struck with their gallantry, " requested that arms might be furnished to them, " when they would set upon them and fight them till " destroyed, but that this butchery of unarmed men " was not the work for sipáhis but the *hullalkhores* " (executioners). Sombre, enraged, struck down those " that objected, and compelled his men to proceed in " their diabolical work until the whole were slain. " The following morning their remains were thrown " into a well in the courtyard. The men employed in " this office found one person, Mr. Gulston of the civil " service, yet alive, and they seemed inclined to save " him; but this gentleman, who was an admirable " linguist, smarting with his wounds, and ignorant of " their kindly intentions towards him, gave them abuse " and threatened them with the vengeance of his " countrymen, upon which they threw him still " breathing into the well with his more fortunate " comrades. A few of the party, probably the sick " and wounded, were in the Chehel Sitún, and were " butchered in a similar manner on the 11th. Neither

" age nor sex was spared, and Sombre consummated " his diabolical villainy by the murder of Mr. Ellis's " infant child, from which it may be inferred that Mrs. " Ellis was amongst the female sufferers in this dreadful " catastrophe." Upwards of fifty civil and military officers and a hundred European soldiers, perished on this occasion. One officer, Dr. Fullarton, whose medical abilities had gained even the regard of Mír Kásim, had been allowed to reside on the Dutch factory, and escaped some days later. Four serjeants also who had been sent for from Purniá by Mír Kásim overpowered the crew of the boat in which they were being conveyed, and escaped.

From this date the fate of Sombre was allied to that of the deadliest enemies of the English. Thenceforward his life was a purgatory. He could expect but one fate should he fall into the hands of the countrymen of his murdered victims. He therefore always carried about with him poison to avoid a catastrophe which he never ceased to dread. Sombre took part in the battle of Patna (May 2nd, 1764), fought by Mír Kásim; and in that of Baksar, fought by the Vizier of Oudh against the English (23rd October, 1764). In both these he displayed his usual shiftiness, retreating on the very suspicion of danger. After the ruin of Mír Kásim (1764) he had transferred himself and his brigade to the Vizier of Oudh, but he left him for the Jâts in August, 1765.

Whilst serving with the Jâts Sombre purchased at Dehli a dancing girl, named Zeb-úl-Nissa, afterwards so notorious as the Bígam Sombre. She has been described as small and plump, with a fair complexion, and large animated eyes. She possessed great talents, the power of influencing others, and was utterly unscrupulous.

After his marriage with Zeb-úl-Nissa Sombre acted on the principle of offering his brigade to the highest bidder. Somehow he always commanded a good price. In 1776 he accepted service under Mirza Najaf Khan, the commander-in-chief of the Moghol army, after having shared in the defeat inflicted by that leader upon his patrons, the Jâts, at Barsána the previous year. The following year the Court of Dehli conferred upon him the principality known as Sirdhána, yielding an annual rental of six lakhs of rupees. This territory was nominally granted to Sombre for the payment of the troops under his command, but upon his death, 4th May, 1778, it passed to Zeb-úl-Nissa, thenceforth known in history as the Bígam Sombre or Samrú.

After Sombre's death the brigade was commanded under the Bígam first by one Pauly, a German who was taken prisoner by Mahomed Beg Hamdání, and executed, in breach of a solemn promise, in 1783. After the murder of Pauly, "three Frenchmen," writes Major L. F. Smith, "Messieurs Baours, Evens, and Dudrenec, successively "commanded and gladly retired." In 1793, the Bígam married her then chief officer, M. Le Vaisseau, "a man "of birth, talents and pride of character,"* who shot

* Major L. F. Smith.

himself two years later. An old and respectable Frenchman, Colonel Saleur, then obtained the command. Under him the brigade increased to six battalions and fought at Assaye, losing there its four guns and many men. The Bígam herself lived till 1836.

Madoc had been a common soldier in the French army. The capture of Chándarnagar in 1757 threw him loose on the country. After some adventures totally unworthy of being recorded, he joined Sombre's brigade, and served under his orders at the several battles in which he was engaged under Mír Kásim. With him he transferred his services in 1764 to the Vizier of Oudh, and obtained at once the command of a separate brigade. At the battle of Baksar he rendered good service. His character was the very opposite of that of Sombre. He was rash, enterprising, and even imprudent. In 1765 he transferred his brigade, which consisted of five battalions, twenty guns, and 500 horse, to the Jâts. Subsequently, and as it suited his purpose, he took service alternately with them, with Mirza Najaf Khan, and with the Ráná of Góhad. In 1776, whilst in alliance with the first-named, he was attacked and his party almost destroyed at Biána by 1500 Rohillas, who surprised him during a storm of rain. On this occasion he lost twelve European officers killed and wounded, all his guns and baggage, and fled, but scantily attended, to Futtehpúr. Thence, however, he made his way to Agra, and succeeded in raising, in an incredibly short space of time, a force as strong in numbers, and as well appointed in men and material as the party he had lost. Receiving shortly afterwards (1782) an offer of a large sum from the Ráná of Góhad for the brigade as it stood, he sold it to him and returned to France. He did not long survive, being killed in a duel. The subsequent life of his brigade was even shorter, Mádhají Sindia, who was then warring with the Ráná, cutting it off to a man in an ambuscade (1784).

V.

It is now time to turn to Raymond.

Michel Joachim Marie Raymond was born at Serignac, the 20th September, 1755. His father was a merchant, and the son followed the same profession. Pushed on by his enterprising nature, however, young Raymond determined to found a corresponding house in India, and with that object he set out in January, 1775, from Lorient for Pondichery, taking with him a large quantity of manufactured goods. He disposed of these to great advantage at Pondichery; then, still drawn on by his ardent nature and his love of adventure, he entered as sub-lieutenant in a corps commanded by the Chevalier de Lassé in the service of Tippú Sahib. With this corps he fought throughout the campaigns of the war which began in 1780 against the English for the possession of Southern India.

When, in March, 1783, the Marquis de Bussy landed in India at the head of 2300 men, one of his first acts was to offer to Raymond, as one who knew the country, the people, and the language, the post of aide-de-camp. Raymond accepted it, and took a share in all the actions under Bussy related in the first book in this volume. Subsequently to the treaty of Versailles, and till the death of Bussy at Pondichery in January, 1785, Raymond occùpied the same post with the rank of captain. But on Bussy's death, he, with the consent of the governor, took service with Nizám Ali Khan, the Súbadár of the Dekhan.

The Súbadárs of the Dekhan had always been partial to the French. It had been under the brother of the Nizám Ali that Bussy with his corps of Frenchmen had gained so great a renown. In July, 1758, Bussy had been compelled, by the policy of Lally, to leave Haidarabád. He then made over charge to M. de Conflans. The following year, however, Conflans surrendered to the English, and the ruler of the Dekhan had been forced not only to renounce the French alliance, but to agree never to permit a French contingent to be quartered within his territories.

This treaty was regarded as binding by Nizám Ali Khan when, in 1761, he imprisoned and succeeded his brother. But there was another brother, Basálat Jang, who held in jaghír from Nizám Ali the district of Gantúr. Basálat considering himself as bound by no treaty, and anxious to have in his service a body of foreigners upon whom he could depend, took into his pay a body of French troops. These were commanded by the younger Lally,* a nephew of the more famous general. Nizám Ali, moved by the English, required

* *Transactions in India.* London, 1786.

his brother to disband this contingent. For five years he refused, and only at last complied when, quarrelling with Haidar Ali, he found it necessary to conciliate the English. Nizám Ali at once took the corps into his own service.

The fate of the younger Lally I have never been able to ascertain, but it is certain that he and the men he commanded were lent in 1779 by the Nizám to Haidar Ali to aid in the prosecution of his war against the English; that they served throughout that war, and on the conclusion of peace returned to Haidarabád.* It seems probable that Lally died or resigned in 1785; certain it is that in that year Raymond succeeded him.

Up to the time of Raymond's arrival at Haidarabád the foreign adventurers who had served his predecessor had constituted one single corps of European cavalry. Simultaneously almost with de Boigne Raymond conceived the idea of improving this system by raising and drilling in the European fashion a considerable body of native troops, who should be commanded, and in part officered, by the adventurers who had survived the then recent campaign.

To this task Raymond bent all his energies. The work was gradual in its accomplishment. It may be asked, perhaps, how the Nizám was able to evade his obligation to the British Government? But this was not difficult. His predecessor had been forbidden to entertain a corps of Frenchmen. This, the Nizám

* *Transactions in India.* London, 1786.

agreed, was not intended to apply, and could not apply, to native battalions officered by foreigners. Notwithstanding, then, the displeasure frequently expressed by the Madras Government, Raymond, under the Nizám's orders, continued to augment the disciplined native troops.

His plan of procedure was different to de Boigne's, and had some advantages over it. These, however, were owing to the larger European material available in his hands. Thus he was able to fix the complement of the European officers to each regiment at eight, of the men at 750.

By the beginning of the year 1795 Raymond had under his command 15,000 disciplined troops, formed into twenty battalions, and officered, including the staff, by 124 Europeans. It was the most formidable body of native troops in the service of a native prince in India. For their support the Nizám assigned to Raymond several districts.

Nevertheless, the first essay of these troops on the field of battle was destined to be unfortunate. In the beginning of 1795 the Nizám, incited by the anarchy prevailing at the Court of Púna, declared war against the Péshwa, and marched to overthrow the Maráthá Empire. The Péshwa summoned his vassals and raised an army to meet him. The two armies met between Kardlá and Parindá, the 12th March, 1795. Raymond had all his men in the field; whilst the Maráthás were aided by twenty-six battalions composed of the men of the brigades of Perron, Filoze, Hessing, Dudrenec, and Boyd. In the sketch of Perron's career I have given an account of the action. It will be seen that not only did Raymond obtain at first an advantage over the Maráthás, but that when the tide turned he covered the retreat, prepared at any moment to convert it into a victory. But for the pusillanimity of the Nizám he might have done so. But with such a leader even a Raymond could not force victory.

During this war with the Maráthás, the Governor General, Lord Teignmouth, had lent the Nizám two battalions of British sepoys to maintain the internal peace of his dominions, while he should concentrate all his forces against the enemy. In doing this Lord Teignmouth had displayed a consideration for the Nizám which might easily have been construed as exceeding the bounds of permissible courtesy, the British being still in alliance with the Péshwa. But even this did not satisfy the Nizám. He wanted active aid; and because he had been refused, he, on the termination of the war, resolved to dispense altogether with British support, and to supply its place by additions to the corps of Raymond. In pursuance of this resolution he, in June, 1795, dismissed the two British battalions. Coincidently with this dismissal he ordered a large increase to Raymond's troops and assigned fresh districts for their maintenance.

But the British troops had scarcely quitted Haidarabád when an event occurred, the effects of which rendered the timorous Nizám more dependent than ever on the allies he was insulting. His eldest son, Ali Jáh, following the family traditions, broke out into rebellion. Quitting the capital under a false pretext the young prince made his way to Bidr, obtained possession of that fortress and of others of less importance, summoned disaffected chiefs and disbanded sepoys to his standard, and was soon able to present a very formidable front to his outraged father.

The first act of Nizám Ali on learning of this revolt was to recall the two British battalions; his second to despatch Raymond against the rebels. Raymond experienced no difficulty. The slightest skirmish sufficed to dissipate the followers of Ali Jáh. The prince fled to Aurangabád, but was pursued and captured. Raymond made over his prisoner to the minister sent by his father to take charge of him. The minister when setting out on his return journey to Haidarabád, directed that the *howdah* in which the prince was seated should be covered with a veil. But Ali Jáh, ashamed of this indignity and afraid to meet his father, took poison and died.

Notwithstanding the suppression of the rebellion, the Nizám still retained the two British regiments at Haidarabád, and he himself fell gradually into a state of dependence on the British Government. This was further evidenced by the difficulties thrown in the way of carrying out the order for the increase of Raymond's corps. The prudent conduct of Raymond at this crisis was not, however, without influence on the mind of his capricious master, and it seems not improbable that, had he lived, all opposition to his schemes would have vanished. He died, however, very suddenly on the 25th March, 1798, just six months prior to the arrival of the crisis which would have tried to the utmost his ability and his influence.

Raymond was a great loss to the enemies of England. No adventurer in India ever stood higher than he did. He was brave, magnificent, generous, affable, and vigilant. To great abilities he united the most consummate prudence. The one dream of his life was to carry out, by the means still open to him, the schemes of Dupleix, of Lally, and of Suffren. He deserves to be ranked with those illustrious warriors in the hierarchy of patriotic Frenchmen. With far fewer means he laid the foundation of a system which excited the greatest apprehension in the minds of the enemies of his country. His death at the early age of forty-four, just as the crisis to which he might have been equal was approaching, was the last drop in the cup of ill-fortune which attended French enterprises in India. It is indeed just possible that his reputation has not suffered from his early demise. Even Raymond might have proved unequal to cope with the great Marquess Wellesley, wielding all the power of British India. But there is this yet to be said of him. No European of mark who preceded him, no European of mark who followed him, in India, ever succeeded in gaining to such an extent, the love, the esteem, the admiration of the natives of the country. The grandsons of the men who loved him then love and revere him now. The hero of the grandfathers is the model warrior of the grandchildren. Round his tomb in the present day there flock still young men and maidens listening to the tales told by the wild dervishes of the great deeds and lofty aspirations of the paladin to whom their sires devoted their fortunes and their lives.

Raymond was succeeded in the command of the French division by M. Piron, a Fleming. Piron was honest, but sadly deficient in prudence. He could not conceal the hatred which he felt towards the English. It happened that Marquess Wellesley had just landed as Governor-General strongly impressed with the designs of General Bonaparte on India, and almost his first act was to require the Nizám to dismiss his French contingent. It is possible that the prudent Raymond might have conjured away or have met the storm. Piron did not possess sufficient character to do either. The Nizám was very unwilling to comply. But he yielded to the pressure put upon him by the great Marquess, and on the 1st September, 1798, he signed a treaty by which he agreed to take no Frenchman in his service, to disband the whole of the infantry lately commanded by Raymond, and to receive in their stead a contingent of British sepoys.

No sooner had the treaty been concluded than four battalions of British sepoys with their guns marched to

Haidarabád, and joined the two battalions formerly stationed there. Some hesitation was even then displayed by the Nizám to break up Piron's corps; but the threatening attitude assumed by the British forced him to issue a proclamation to his disciplined sepoys informing them that their French officers were dismissed. The scene that followed was remarkable. These sepoys had adored Raymond; they had looked to their European officers with affection and pride; they would have followed them to the end of the earth; they knew that their dismissal was due, not to the wish of the Nizám, but to British influence. On hearing, then, the proclamation of the Nizám, they first murmured, then broke out into rebellion. But their European officers had been secured; their cantonments had been surrounded; from every point they saw their position commanded by cannon. Resistance being then hopeless, they surrendered, asking each other with a sigh: "Would this have been, had "Raymond only lived?" The French officers were sent to France.

I have now brought to a close this sketch of the careers of the principal foreign adventurers who flourished in India between the signature of the treaty of Versailles and the fatal blow dealt to the Maráthá Empire by Marquess Wellesley in 1803-4. From that moment the British Empire in India was secure. Thenceforth neither native prince nor foreign adventurer could stay its onward progress. Any war which might break out, from the Satlaj down to the sea, could cause no serious disquiet to the Governor-General of British India. Even the acute sovereign of the warlike clan which had established a powerful monarchy beyond the Satlaj—even Ranjit Singh foresaw the doom which awaited even the kingdom he had created. "It will all," he said, as he noted on the map the red border which encircled the various provinces already under British sway, "it will all become red." His words were a prophecy. The impetus given to the vast machine could not be stopped until the final goal had been attained. The various, so to speak, indigenous races which had tried to found an empire in India had failed. The Hindús, brave as they were, became to a great extent demoralised by an over-refinement of civilisation; an over-refinement which, amongst other strange forms, made of food a religion. This one law, this article of faith, which prevents combination, restricts men to a certain diet, to be partaken of only under certain fixed conditions, is sufficient in the present day to prevent the race which practises it from holding the chief sway over such a country as Hindostan. The northern warriors who ruled on their ruin had defects of an opposite character not less fatal to permanent predominance. With some brilliant exceptions they were intolerant, and the security—the very existence even—of their rule always depended on the character of the ruler. The Maráthás, who succeeded them, were in every sense of the word adventurers—fortune hunters who rose from nothing, men of neither birth, position, nor descent—

the marauders which a country in the last throes of its agony sends out from its lurking places to plunder and destroy. Such was Síváji; such were the earlier representatives of the Gáikwár, of Sindia, of Holkar, and of the Bhónslá. Yet these men founded an empire. The Maráthás succeeded the Moghols. When Lord Lake entered Dehli, in 1803, the men he had beaten beneath its walls were the soldiers of the greatest of the Maráthá chieftains. Virtually he restored the Moghol.

Could the Maráthá Empire have lasted if there had been no foreign power on the spot to supplant it? To those who would pause for a reply I would point to the condition of the Court of Púna after the death of the Péshwa, Madhú Ráo Narain, in 1795. It was the Court of Dehli after the demise of a sovereign in its worst days. It was the Court of Dehli as it always was after the death of Aurangzib. The Maráthá system of rule was cursed with the same inherent vice which was the bane of the Moghol sway. The succession was never secure to any one member of the family. The people were never safe against the exactions of their rulers. The rulers were never safe against treachery and insurrection. The inevitable consequences were intrigue, rapine, slaughter, constant wars, incessant oppression of the people. Had there been no foreigners on the spot to supplant the Maráthá rule, it is probable that the various members of its clan would have fought to a standstill, only in the end to make way for some new invader from the north—possibly, for the moment, for Ranjit Singh—to relapse, on his death, into renewed anarchy.

It would seem, then, to have been necessary for the safety of India that the successor to the Maráthá should be a foreigner. Who was that foreigner to be? It was inevitable that he should come from Europe, for the children of northern Asia had been tried and found wanting. Portugal made the first venture, ignorant of the possible stake she might be called to play for. Holland, with a keener, though still very dim appreciation of the future, followed and, in part, supplanted Portugal. Then came England with a vision more clouded than that of Holland, caring nothing for dominion, looking only for gain. Last of all stepped in France. To the brilliant intellect of her gifted sons the nature of the mission which lay before one European power was not for long a sealed book. The greatest of the children whom she sent to India, recognising the priceless value of the stake, risked his all to win it. Had the Bourbon who ruled France properly supported him he would have won it. As it was the intensity of the passion he displayed in playing the great game communicated some vague idea of its importance to his English rivals. The genius of Clive clutched it; the statesmanlike brain of Warren Hastings nurtured it; the commanding intellect of Marquess Wellesley established it as an ineradicable fact. Yet, throughout this period, France, which had been the first to conceive the idea never resigned it. She had much to contend against. The narrow visions of her monarch and her statesmen could not grasp the vital importance of the mighty stake. It was these men who prevented India from becoming French. I have but to point to a few instances of their incapacity. The restoration of Madras by the peace of Aix la Chapelle; the recall of Dupleix, when if they had sent him but one regiment more, he would have gained southern India; the diminution of the forces ordered to be sent with Lally; the appointment as his colleague of such a man as d'Aché; the acknowledgment by the treaty of Versailles of the *status quo ante bellum*, when the English were reduced to their last grasp in southern India; all these were fatal errors due to that want of comprehensive grasp which marked the statesmen of the later Bourbons. Frenchmen on the spot, indeed, atoned nobly for the errors of their rulers. They fought for the idea, as long as it could be fought for; and when they beheld it slipping from their grasp they yet struggled with skill, with courage, and with pertinacity to prevent its appropriation by their rivals. In my history of the French in India, not less than in this volume, I have endeavoured to draw a vivid and a true picture of their aims and of their struggles. Those aims were worthy of being recorded, for they were lofty; those struggles deserved a historian, for they were gallant. The record reveals to us, moreover, this great people displaying qualities for which the world has not given them credit. We all knew that the French were clever, brave, and venturesome. Not every one, however, is prepared to find in a Frenchman the long pertinacity displayed by Dupleix; the quality of not knowing when he was beaten evinced by Suffren; the daring hardihood of her privateersmen; or lastly, the patience, the energy, the perseverance shown under trying circumstances by some of the adventurers whose deeds have been recorded in this book. England, who, grasping gradually the idea of France, now occupies the position to which a Frenchman first aspired, only does honour to herself when she recognises the splendid qualities displayed by her most formidable rival; allows that on the sea as well as on land she met a worthy antagonist; and admits, that if for the favourable result of the contest she owes much to the genius and the comprehensive views of the great statesmen who guided the councils of her country during a large portion of the eighteenth century, she is indebted even to a greater extent to the errors committed by the statesmen of the enemy she was combating.

APPENDIX.

THE BRITISH EXPEDITION FROM INDIA TO EGYPT IN 1801.

On the 5th February, 1801, Major-General David Baird, at the time commanding the Dinapore division, received orders to repair at once to Trincomali, there to assume the command of a force assembled with the object of capturing the island of Java, and, on the completion of that task, of attempting the reduction of the isles of France and Bourbon.

The force to be employed on this service consisted of the 10th, 19th, and 80th regiments of the line, of detachments from the 86th and 88th, of a Corps of Bengal Native Volunteers, and of two companies of European and Native Artillery with lascars attached.

The most minute instructions regarding the movements of the force had been detailed by Marquess Wellesley. After Java should have been captured

General Baird, was to remain there as Lieutenant-Governor, whilst his second in command, Colonel the Honourable Arthur Wellesley, should proceed towards the islands.

The same day, the 5th February, General Baird embarked on board the Honourable Company's ship *Phœnix*, but before that vessel had left the Saugor roads, Marquess Wellesley received a despatch from the President of the Board of Control, the effect of which was to entirely alter the destination of the expedition.

In that despatch Mr. Dundas informed the Governor-General, that Sir Ralph Abercromby had received orders to proceed up the Mediterranean and, by an attack on Alexandria and the coast, to co-operate with the Turkish army assembling in Syria, in whatever plan might be concerted with them for expelling the French army from Egypt; and that it had been thought expedient "that a " force should be sent also from India to act in such a " manner as might appear conducive to that essential " object," from the side of the Red Sea.

Mr. Dundas added that, with that object in view Sir Home Popham, with a proper squadron, would be immediately sent into that sea, taking with him a regiment from the Cape of Good Hope; that his first rendezvous would be the Port of Mocha; and he directed that a force of about 1000 Europeans and 2000 Native Infantry should be sent at once from India to the proposed place of rendezvous, with as little delay as possible, to co-operate with Sir Home Popham.

Copies of this despatch were sent to the presidencies of Madras and Bombay, the Governors of which were instructed to make the necessary preparations without delay, and even to carry the orders into execution without waiting for the Governor-General's directions, if they were ready in other respects.

The despatch concluded by expressing a belief that unless anything unforeseen should occur the armament under Sir Ralph Abercromby would reach the coast of Egypt in December, and that of Sir H. Popham would arrive at its destination in the February following. The Governor-General was therefore earnestly recommended to despatch the Indian Contingent as quickly as possible; not even to wait till the troops should all be collected if it would save time to forward them in two or three distinct detachments.

Lord Wellesley received this despatch,—dated the 6th October, 1800, and forwarded overland—on the 6th February. The same day he intimated to General Baird that a despatch from England would probably render it necessary for him to make some essential variations in the object of the armament he had equipped; that meanwhile General Baird had better remain on board the *Phœnix*, urging the captain, however, to make every necessary preparation for sailing, as he hoped to send the further instructions within forty-eight hours.

But it was not till the 10th that the Military Secretary to the Governor-General intimated to General Baird, in a short note, that the despatch from England had rendered it necessary that he should "assist Sir Ralph "Abercromby in driving the French from Egypt instead "of seizing on Batavia." The same evening Marquess Wellesley forwarded his instructions, accompanied by a very friendly letter, to General Baird.

These instructions and letters were received by General Baird on the afternoon of the 13th The *Phœnix* sailed the same day for Trincomali ; but before she reached her destination events had occurred to which it is now necessary to refer.

Colonel Wellesley, appointed second in command of the expedition against Java and the islands, was already at Trincomali when a copy of Mr. Dundas's despatch of the 6th October reached the Madras Government. This copy was at once forwarded to Colonel Wellesley who determined, in consequence, to proceed at once with the troops under his command (excepting the 19th regiment for which he could not procure tonnage) to Bombay, and thence to the place of rendezvous pointed out in the despatches from Mr. Dundas. He accordingly embarked with the troops from Ceylon on the 14th February.

Colonel Wellesley reached Bombay about the middle of March. He at once communicated with the Governor, and sent off to Mocha a detachment of Bombay troops under the command of Colonel Ramsay of the 80th Regiment. He then set to work to prepare transports for a second detachment, and the progress in this respect had been considerable when General Baird, who, on missing him at Trincomali, had pushed on in the *Wasp* gun-vessel, joined him on the 31st March.

So indefatigable, indeed, had been the exertions of Colonel Wellesley that on the 3rd April the second detachment of the force, under the command of Colonel Beresford of the 88th Regiment, was able to sail in six transports from Bombay. On that very day Colonel Wellesley was attacked by intermittent fever, and on the 5th the medical officers declared that it would be utterly impossible for him to sail then with the expedition, though he might possibly be able to follow in time to catch up the second division.

This second division consisted of the troops which General Baird had found at Trincomali and which had started from that port for Mocha.

General Baird himself left Bombay on the 6th April and reached Mocha on the 24th. On his arrival there he found that Colonel Murray, who had been despatched to that place several months before, had sailed for Jedda on the 17th, having on the 12th sent on Colonel Ramsay's detachment. He found likewise that Colonel Beresford's detachment had arrived on the 21st and sailed again on the 24th.

General Baird, fearing lest these two detachments uniting at Jedda might make a premature attempt upon Kosseir, which place, in default of Suez, unapproachable at that season by sailing ships, he had designed as his base of operations, sent off directions to Colonels Murray and Beresford to remain at Jedda until he should join them with another detachment under Lieutenant-Colonel Montresor of the 80th Regiment. That detachment reached Mocha on the 28th April. Leaving at that place despatches detailing the arrangement he had decided upon for Colonel Champagné, commanding the detachment still due, for Colonel Wellesley, and for Sir Home Popham (expected from England), General Baird set out for Jedda with Colonel Montresor's division on the 30th.

He reached Jedda on the 18th May. There he found that his despatches had arrived too late to be communicated to Colonel Murray; that that officer, taking with him the Bombay detachment under Colonel Ramsay and the division under Colonel Beresford, had sailed up the Gulf towards Suez. Baird's first impulse was to follow them; but he was restrained by the necessity which existed to take in a supply of fresh water—the tanks having run very low. He availed himself of the delay thus caused to endeavour to secure by every means in his power the friendship and co-operation of the chief authorities at Mecca.

On the evening of his arrival, Baird received intelligence of the victory gained on the 21st March by Sir Ralph Abercromby over the French troops under General Menou.

On the 24th General Baird was on the point of sailing from Jedda when Sir Home Popham arrived in H.M.S. *Romney*, 50 guns, with the sloop *Victor* in company, closely followed by the division he was escorting from the Cape. This consisted of H.M.'s 61st Regiment, commanded by Lieutenant-Colonel Carruthers; several troops of the 8th Light Dragoons, Captain Hawkers; and a detachment, Royal Artillery, Captain Beaver. Sir Home Popham brought, however, no intelligence regarding Colonels Wellesley and Champagné. Nothing had been heard at Mocha either of them or of the provision ships that were to precede or accompany them when Sir Home Popham touched at that place.

On the 26th May Baird sailed from Jedda with Sir Home Popham in the *Romney*, and reached Kosseir on the 6th June. He found there Colonel Murray, and the troops that had accompanied them.

The force then under his orders was composed as follows:—

Royal Artillery	...	Captain Beaver.
Bengal Horse Do.	...	Captain Browne.
Bengal Foot Do.	...	Captain Fleming.
Madras Do. Do.	...	Major Bell.
Bombay Do. Do.	...	Captain Powell.
Royal Engineers.		
Bengal Do.		
Madras Do.		
Bombay Do.		
Madras Pioneers.		
H.M.'s 8th Light Dragoons	...	Captain Hawkers.
,, 10th Foot	...	Lt.-Col. Quarril.
,, 61st Foot	...	Lt.-Col. Carruthers.
,, 80th Foot	...	Colonel Ramsay.
,, 86th Foot	...	Lt.-Col. Lloyd.
,, 88th Foot	...	Colonel Beresford.
Bengal Volunteer N. I.	...	Captain Michie.
1st Bombay Regt. N. I.	...	Major Holmes.
7th Do. Do.	...	Major Laureston.

The respective quota furnished by the different establishments to which these corps belonged is thus to be divided:—

		Men.
East India Company's Artillery	...	448
Do. Do. Native Troops	...	1940
H.M's. Troops	...	2438
Total	...	4826

To these must be added—

European officers	218
Native ditto	53
Drummers	125
Lascars	440
Servants not soldiers	276
Public followers	572
Private ditto	305
Grand Total ...	6815

This force was commanded in chief by Major-General David Baird, 54th Foot, who had as his Adjutant-General, Colonel Achmuty, 10th Foot, and as Quarter-Master-General, Colonel Murray, 84th Foot. It was divided into two brigades the Right and the Left, the former commanded by Colonel Beresford, the latter bý Lieutenant-Colonel Montresor.

General Baird's first act, after arriving at Kosseir, was to place himself in the communication with General Hely Hutchinson, commanding the British Army of Egypt after the death of Sir Ralph Abercromby. But his letter had been sent off only five days, when he received a despatch from General Hutchinson himself dated the 13th May, from Rahamenie on the Nile.

In this letter General Hutchinson stated that it was his intention to push on towards Cairo so as to prevent the French from attacking the Indian force before it should have effected its junction with the Grand Vizier; that he had written to that high officer to give General Baird all the assistance he might require for the passage of the desert.

After alluding generally to the difficulties to be encountered from the climate and the people General Hutchinson added that he intended to continue in his position near Cairo until he should hear that the Indian force was in a state of security; that he would then descend the Nile and besiege Alexandria; that he rather opined that General Baird should join the army of the Grand Vizier and besiege Cairo with him, for which purpose he would endeavour to procure for him some heavy artillery as none could be brought across the desert.

To this letter General Baird replied that the Admiral on the station (Admiral Blankett) had pronounced the journey by sea to Suez at that season of the year to be impossible; and that he was about to send off his Quarter-Master-General, Colonel Murray, to Keneh, where he would either remain, or proceed down the Nile to open a communication with General Hutchinson.

General Baird, in anticipation of a forward movement had already established military posts for nearly half the distance between Kosseir and Keneh, and had directed the men forming them to dig for water. At all these posts water had been found. The General determined therefore to push on a corps at once in advance, to be followed by others. The first of these corps commanded by Colonel Beresford left Kosseir, therefore, on the 19th June.

The route they had to take may thus be concisely shewn :*

* This itinerary is taken from the official orders signed by Colonel Montresor and compiled after General Baird had himself made the journey between the two places. The list given in the Memoirs of Sir

	Miles.	
Kosseir to the New Wells...	11	Water.
Half way to Moilah ...	17	No water.
To Moilah	17	Water & provisions.
Advanced Wells	9	Water.
Half way to Legeta ...	19	No water.
To Legeta	19	Water & provisions.
To Baromba	18	Water.
To Keneh, on the Nile ...	10	The Nile.
Total	120	

The march was encumbered with difficulties. The very first day many of the water bags leaked so much that all the water had escaped before the troops reached their destination; the wells which had been dug there yielded indeed water, but it was procurable only in very small quantities. The dreariness of the country; the depressing nature of the climate; the burning sand and the burning sun; all these added to the difficulties of the General, and called for the exercise of all his firmness, his presence of mind, and his fortitude.

General Baird had accompanied the two first detachments a part of the way. He then returned to Kosseir to arrange measures for providing a water supply for the troops forming them. He had previously succeeded in obtaining about 5000 camels, and these he loaded with leathern bags or *mashaks*. In an order which he issued on the occasion will be found the means he had assertained to be most efficacious for supplying the troops on the line of march with this necessary article.

David Baird was written before the journey had been attempted, and is incomplete and imperfect. *Vide Asiatic Annual Register* for 1802.

After examining the various modes which had been suggested for ensuring a regular water-supply he announced the conclusion at which he had arrived that the army "must either trust to the puckallies, or find water "in the desert, or re-embark."

The order then proceeded as follows: "To-day's "march of the 88th will decide the first point, and if "it is possible to carry water it should be done in this "way.

"The 88th should take their bags on to Legeta, and "after the next day's march thence, send them back to "Legeta for the next corps.

"The 10th should take their bags to Moilah, and "after the next day's march send their bags back to "Moilah for the next division. The artillery, increased "to 100 puckallie camels, should take their bags one "day's march to the wells, and send them back. By "these three divisions of bags the whole army could, in "succession, be supplied. Careful, steady men should "be appointed to each division, and the principle should "be well explained to everybody. A European officer "should also go with each division of puckallies.

"If the puckallies will not answer and the 88th get "on to Moilah, a company should be sent to clear the "wells, seven miles from Moilah, and two companies "should be sent halfway from that towards Legeta to "dig wells, and, as fast as they find water, more com-"panies should follow.

"In the same manner the 10th should send two "companies halfway to Moilah and endeavour to dig "wells.

"If water is found at these stations, the 88th must

"halt at Legeta, and send on two companies to dig "wells between that and Keneh.

"The Sepoys at the stations may go and assist, and "the two companies at Legeta should immediately "begin between that and Keneh."

General Baird had decided to leave Kosseir for Keneh on the 27th June. On that day, however, he received despatches from Bombay informing him that Colonel Champagné's detachment would sail in six transports "in a few days," and that Colonel Wellesley was prevented by ill health from joining him.

A feeling of soreness had existed between General Baird and Colonel Wellesley since the date (5th May, 1799) on which the former had considered himself superseded by the latter in the command of Seringapatam. It is interesting, therefore, to read the manner in which an ill-feeling on the part of Colonel Wellesley had been effaced by personal contact with General Baird in Bombay.

"As I am writing on the subject," wrote Colonel Wellesley in a private letter dated Bombay, 9th April, "I will freely acknowledge that my regret at being "prevented from accompanying you has been greatly "increased by the kind, candid, and handsome manner "in which you have behaved towards me; and I will "confess as freely, not only that I did not expect such "treatment, but that my wishes, before you arrived, "regarding going upon such an expedition, were "directly the reverse of what they are at this moment. "I need not enter farther into this subject than to "entreat that you will not attribute my stay to any "other motive than that to which I have above "assigned it"—(the state of his health)—"and to "inform you that, as I know what has been said and "expected by the world in general, I propose, as "well as for my own credit as for yours, to make "known to my friends and to yours, not only the "distinguished manner in which you have behaved "towards me, but the causes which have prevented my "demonstrating my gratitude by giving you every "assistance in the arduous service which you have to "conduct."

Colonel Wellesley accompanied his letter by a memorandum in which he detailed the course he would recommend the general in command of the force invading Egypt from India to adopt.

Dismissing as impracticable any attempt to gain Suez in sailing ships at that season of the year, Colonel Wellesley indicated Kosseir as the place of which the army should first gain possession.

After referring to the probable movements of the French troops, and the disposition of the Mamelukes and the Beys, the memorandum thus proceeded:—

"The first question which I shall consider, and which "will lay the grounds for a consideration of, and "decision upon others, is whether it would be prac-"ticable or even desirable to cross the desert from "Kosseir at all, if that operation is not performed in "concert and co-operation with a body of natives posted "upon the Nile.

"It is needless to enter into a statement of the "difficulties to be apprehended in crossing the desert; "they are certainly great, but I imagine not insur-"mountable. But, if it is not certain that the army or "detachment which will cross the desert, will partake "of the plenty of the banks of the Nile when they "reach them; if they should be certain of having water "only, and such forage as their cattle should be able to "pick up, I apprehend that the difficulty will become "so great that the operation ought not to be attempted. "It is impossible that the Mamelukes in Upper Egypt "can be neutral in the contest in contemplation—they "must take part with the French or with us. If they "take part with the French, the army will be in the "situation in which I have above described it, enjoying "no advantage from having reached the banks of the "Nile, excepting water, and probably some forage; "and it is needless to point out that if the desert is to "be crossed under those circumstances care must be "taken not only to send, with the body of troops which "will cross, a very large proportion of provisions, but "means must be adopted to add to them until the "operations of this body shall have given them such a "hold of the country as to leave no doubt of their "steady supply of provisions. It is obvious that this "will require a great number of cattle, a number much "larger than the Government of India, with all the "zealous exercise of their power and means, can supply; "but there is another consideration connected with this "subject besides the supply of cattle, and that is "the means of feeding them when landed from the ships.

"Upon this point I need only call to the General's "recollection the difficulties to which he has been a "witness in moving large supplies of stores and pro- "visions even in fertile, cultivated, and inhabited

" countries, well supplied with water, and under every " disadvantage of arrangement in the supply, in the " distribution, and the food of the cattle, and draw a " comparison between such difficulties and those to be " expected in a march through a desert. But that is " not the worst that is to be apprehended; the cattle " will of course land in a weak condition, in a desert, " and it must be expected that even those which survive " the voyage will starve or at least be in such a state " before they commence their march as to render it " very probable that they will not carry their loads to " the end of it. Upon the whole, then, I am decidedly " of opinion that if the Mamelukes are not on our side, " no attempt ought to be made to cross the desert.

" This opinion, the General will observe, is by no " means founded on the impracticability of crossing " with troops, because I am convinced that it can be " done; but it is founded upon the danger that the " troops will starve if they do not return immediately, " and upon the inutility of the measure if they do.

" It may be imagined that (supposing the Mamelukes " to be wavering) if an attempt is not made to cross the " desert, the advantage of their co-operation will be " lost. Upon this point I observe, that a knowledge " of our strength (not of our weakness) will induce them " to come forward, and it might be expected that the " sight of our weakness, occasioned by our march over " the desert without concert with them, might induce " them to take advantage of it and to join the French.

" But those who will urge this consideration must " suppose it possible that the Mamelukes can be " neutral for a moment; and this, their history from

" the beginning of time, particularly since the French " invasion, will show to be impossible.

"I come now to consider the propriety and mode of " crossing the desert, supposing that the Mamelukes " should be inclined to shake off the French yoke and to " co-operate with us. The first point for the General " to ascertain is their sincerity in the cause, of which, " as I have above stated, there is every probability. As " soon as he will have ascertained this, it will be " necessary that he should make arrangements with " them for posting a supply of water on that part of " the desert where it is most wanted, and for having a " supply of provisions ready on the Nile; and he might " cross over a part of his army immediately. The first " object on his arrival on the Nile should be to estab- " lish a post at Keneh, and, if possible, another in the " desert between that place and Kosseir, in order to " insure his communications between the sea and the " Nile. At Keneh he should make the depôt of his " stores, &c., which might be brought across the desert " by degrees, and then he might commence his " operations against the enemy.

"In the consideration of the question regarding the " crossing of the desert I have omitted to mention the " interruption which may be given to that operation by " the enemy, because it is entirely distinct from the " difficulties which are peculiar to the operation itself. " It is obvious, however, that if the Mamelukes are not " on our side, and if they should not have driven out " of Upper Egypt the small French force supposed to " be in that country before the operation is attempted, " that force, however small, will greatly increase the "distress of the British troops who will cross the desert. "I have not adverted to the supply of arms and "ammunition to be given to the natives. As long "as their co-operation is doubtful these supplies ought "to be withheld but promised; when they will have "shown their sincerity in our cause, the arms may be "given to almost any extent."

On the third day after the receipt of this memorandum, viz., the 30th June, General Baird quitted Kosseir. He had calculated that it would take him ten days to concentrate all his force at Keneh. Thence, should he be able to collect a sufficient number of boats, it might be possible for him to reach Cairo in twenty days. On the other hand, the land march from Keneh to Cairo would take, he believed, thirty-five days.

The difficulties of the march, owing to the want of water, the heat, and the trying character of the soil, and the obstacles in the way of communication, were so great that General Baird, lion-hearted as he was, despaired, whilst waiting at Keneh for orders, of being able to effect anything useful to the public service. For many days he was without intelligence of, and received no orders from, General Hutchinson. Under these circumstances, and dreading lest the breaking out of the monsoon might interfere with his return to India, he, on the 9th July, addressed from Keneh to H.R.H. the Duke of York, a letter expressive of his anxiety to know whether his continuance in Egypt was likely to be productive of any beneficial results to the service.

Just at this moment intelligence reached General Baird, by a circuitous route, that General Belliard, the French Governor of Cairo, had entered into a treaty with General Hutchinson. This information convinced General Baird that there could be no longer any necessity for his further advance, still less for bringing up more troops. Penetrated by this idea, he directed preparations to be made for the return of the force then at Keneh to Kosseir, and for its embarkation at the latter place.

But a few days latter these views were destined to be altered. About the 22nd July General Baird received from General Hutchinson a letter, dated the 10th idem, in which that officer, after alluding to the want of information under which he had been labouring as to the strength and destination of the Indian force, stated that the French Commander-in-Chief, General Menou, had refused to receive the officer sent by General Belliard to lay before him the capitulation of Cairo, and that it was probable that he would defend himself with great obstinacy and give a great deal of trouble; that he should be extremely glad, therefore, to have General Baird's assistance and co-operation.

As to the mode of his advance and the means he should employ to effect it, General Hutchinson thus expressed himself: "I am thoroughly aware that from " the season, and from the inundation, the march by land " will be impracticable. You must do all you can to " collect boats, but whether you should use force or not " is entirely out of the question, beeause, for the last " thousand years force has been the only law in this " country, and the inhabitants are so little used to think " for themselves that they are at a great loss how to act " when it is not adopted against them."

He added, "I wish you to advance as soon as you

"conveniently can without pressing or fatiguing your "troops; you may march by detachments, and let "them be ever so small there can be no difficulty in "making your rendezvous at Gizeh which I have "occupied entirely for your convenience. You have "only to intimate your wishes to Colonel Stewart" (Commandant of Gizeh) "and everything will be "procured for you that the country affords."

With respect to his own movements General Hutchinson stated that his army had marched on the 9th and would arrive at Rosetta about the 29th. Thence he intended to proceed without loss of time to besiege Alexandria.

On receiving this letter General Baird lost no time in ordering all the troops up from Kosseir. Amongst those who responded to his call were four companies of the 61st Regiment, two of the 80th, the Horse Artillery from Bengal, and the Artillery and Pioneers from Madras,—recently arrived at Kosseir. I may mention that Colonel Champagné and the provision ships had not even then arrived; and that the *Susannah*, the ship in which Colonel Arthur Wellesley was to have sailed, was lost on her passage! Never certainly was an attack of fever more opportune than that which prevented the future conqueror of Napoleon from taking part in this expedition.

On the 24th July General Baird despatched Colonel Quarrill with the 10th Regiment to Girgeh with instructions to enquire, on his arrival there, into the state of the roads and of the inundations; he was further directed, that if he should find he could with safety proceed to Siout or to any town capable of furnishing adequate supplies for his troops, to march thither, and thence proceed in a similar manner as rapidly as he could towards Cairo, taking care never to expose himself to the chance of being overtaken by the flooding of the Nile at any considerable distance from a large town.

Colonel Quarrill was farther instructed, if he should find the roads impassable, to select some high ground, and wait the arrival of the river fleet with the General.

Having sent off Colonel Quarrill, General Baird proceeded to impress or otherwise procure boats. This was an easy task, and it was soon ascertained that the supply would exceed the demand. These boats were of three sizes. One of the largest size was capable of carrying 150 men, three field officers, a proportion of officers junior to that rank, and their servants; a medium-sized boat would contain 120 men; and a small boat thirty-five. It is stated that the 88th Regiment, consisting of 590 men and officers, with eight horses, took up seven boats of the different sizes above enumerated.

Having made all his preparations General Baird, appointing Colonel Murray to the command of the troops in Upper Egypt, and instructing him to remain at Keneh until the rear of the army should have come up and been sent on to Gizeh, embarked for that place on the 31st July.

Gizeh was reached on the 8th August. After having arranged for the comfort of his troops the General, on the 16th, shifted his quarters to Rhoda, a little island, a mile and three-quarters long and one third of a mile broad situated between Gizeh and Cairo, and two miles from the latter. On the 27th having left a force under

Colonel Ramsay to garrison Gizeh, he concentrated all his troops in the island.

It may not be out of place here to notice the effect which the sight of the Anglo-Indian army produced upon the Egyptians and Turks. The following passage extracted from the *Asiatic Annual Register* for 1802 may be accepted as giving an impartial view on the subject. "Whilst at Rhoda," writes the chronicler "the Indian Army had attracted much surprise and "admiration. The Turks were astonished at the novel "spectacle of men of colour being so well disciplined "and trained. Indeed the general magnificence of the "establishment of the Indian army was so different "from what they had been accustomed to see in "General Hutchinson's that the contrast could not "fail of being striking. But General Baird proved "to them also that his troops were not enfeebled or "himself rendered inactive, by these superior comforts. "Every morning at day-light he manœuvred his army "for several hours, and in the evening again formed "his parade. Never were finer men seen than those "which composed this force, and no soldiers could "possibly be in higher order."

On the night of the 27th August the right wing of the army began to move in the direction of Alexandria and, with General Baird at its head, reached Rosetta on the 30th. A detachment under Colonel Lloyd was about the same time sent to garrison Damietta, but in consequence of a difference of opinion with the Grand Vizier, commanding the Turkish army, it was withdrawn, the European portion of it being sent to Rosetta, and the native (four companies Bombay N. I.) to Gizeh.

On arriving at Rosetta General Baird and his force hoped to be able to take part in the siege of Alexandria, but their ardour was damped by the receipt of a letter from General Hutchinson, announcing that the French had sent a flag of truce to him to treat for a surrender. General Baird was ordered to halt where he was.

On the 1st September General Baird called upon General Hutchinson in his tent. He learned from him that the capitulation had been actually signed and that the British troops were to take possession of the outworks of Alexandria the following morning.

The Anglo-Indian army then disembarked and encamped at Aboumandur, not far from Rosetta.

For some months the Indian army remained encamped near Rosetta without orders either from England or from India. Meanwhile a difficulty arose. General Hutchinson had resolved to proceed to England, and the British Government had replaced him by Lord Cavan. This officer declined to look upon General Baird as commanding a separate force distinct from the British army, but desired to place him and his troops in the same alignment, as it were, as the troops who had come direct from England. To this General Baird objected, assigning as one great obstacle to the success of such an arrangement the fact that the troops under his orders received Indian rates of pay, and that the money he had to dispose of as commanding the Indian expedition was the property, not of the Crown, but of the East India Company. General Hutchinson appeared to see great force in these objections; but he did not the less, on his departure, the 6th November, make over command of the whole army, including the Anglo-Indian force, to Lord Cavan.

Shortly after this intelligence arrived of the signing of the preliminaries of peace between France and England, and, at nearly the same time, General Baird received from Marquess Wellesley a despatch, in which, whilst expressing full approval of his conduct, he intimated a wish that when the services of the army should be no longer required in Egypt, General Baird should return with his troops, or at least with such portion of them as it might not be necessary to leave in Egypt, to the nearest port in India.

On the 30th April, 1802, despatches were received from England directing that the native troops, and a portion of the European troops on the Indian establishment serving in Egypt, should return at once to India by sea from Suez.

General Baird at once made the necessary preparations for evacuating the country. He ordered parties to be sent from Gizeh, to be stationed along the desert, in order to dig for water. He himself left Alexandria for Gizeh on the 7th May, and arrived at that place on the 11th. He set out thence, after an interview with the Pasha, at the head of his troops, for Suez, which place he reached on the 25th. The troops crossed the desert in successive divisions, in five easy marches each, without experiencing much inconvenience, and with the loss of only three Europeans.

On the 5th June, General Baird and his army left Suez. The ship on which he himself was on board, H.M.S. *Victor*, reached Madras the 6th July, and Calcutta the 31st idem. On that day the Governor-

General published a congratulatory General Order, in which he made special allusion to the terms in which Lord Cavan had written regarding the Anglo-Indian force. As the language used was the result of personal experience during a considerable time, of a force serving under his own orders, I propose here to reproduce it.

Lord Cavan, alluding to the Anglo-Indian force, wrote :—" Their excellent discipline and obedience and " their patience under great fatigue and hardship, have " been equalled by their exemplary conduct in the " correct and regular discharge of every duty of soldiers; " and, though they may lament that circumstances " rendered it impossible for them to have taken part in " the brilliant actions of this country during the last " campaign, it must be a satisfaction for them to know " that their services in Egypt have been as important, " and as essential to their country, as those of their " brother soldiers that gained such distinguished vic- " tories in it."

I do not think I can better conclude than by this testimony of the Commander-in-Chief of the Army of Egypt to the character and conduct of his two Indian Brigades this short narrative of the Anglo-Indian expedition to Egypt of 1801.

INDEX.

LONDON: